AF540923

Communicative Method in ELT

An Indian Perspective

Communicative Method in ELT

An Indian Perspective

Mubeena Fazili

Published by

ATLANTIC

PUBLISHERS & DISTRIBUTORS (P) LTD

7/22, Ansari Road, Darya Ganj,
New Delhi-110002
Phones : +91-11-40775252, 23273880, 23275880, 23280451
Fax : +91-11-23285873
Web : www.atlanticbooks.com
E-mail : orders@atlanticbooks.com

Branch Office
5, Nallathambi Street, Wallajah Road,
Chennai-600002
Phones : +91-44-64611085, 32413319
E-mail : chennai@atlanticbooks.com

Printed in India at Glorious Printers, A-13, D.S.I.D.C.,
Jhilmil Industrial Area, Delhi-110095

Dedicated
with love and affection
to my parents whose
blessings made me
achieve my goal.

Preface

The book, as the name implies, deals mainly with methodology in teaching and various issues related to it such as syllabus design, classroom techniques and testing and evaluation. The book is published with a view to providing an insight into our existing language teaching. All aspects of Language Teaching and Testing have been discussed in detail. Various problems faced by teachers and students like unmanageable class roll, limited time, lengthy syllabus, lack of proper planning of the causes, unspecified aims and objectives of the curriculum, unrealistic materials (not related to real-life situations), outdated methods of teaching, faulty testing techniques and lack of feedback have all been discussed thoroughly, and possible practical solutions suggested. Responses have been sought from both teachers and students of various colleges which all testify to the fact that our language teaching is defective and needs a change.

A whole new curriculum with a learner-centred focus has been suggested. Problems likely to be faced on its implementation have been envisaged and remedial solutions given. The book therefore would be of great help to researchers, scholars and syllabus framers, besides being a reference book for students of education.

MUBEENA FAZILI

Contents

Preface vii

Introduction 1

1. The Communicative Methodology in English Language Teaching: Past and Present 5

2. Communicative Method in Teaching English for Non-Native Environments 36

3. The Present Indian Scenario: An Analysis of the Data Collected 79

4. Implementation of the Communicative Method in our Situation 104

Conclusion 138

Appendices 141

Bibliography 183

Introduction

English has been taught in our educational institutions for quite sometime now, yet our students feel handicapped in using it effectively in and outside their classrooms. The reasons are many and manifold but the most obvious and glaring is the use of faulty methods of teaching and learning the language at various levels of our education. The methods so far used have been the Grammar-Translation and the Direct Method or at best an 'Eclectic Method' which combines some characteristics of both. These methods consider language learning/teaching a mechanical process without considering its cognitive aspects. The learner is considered a mere appendage in the learning/teaching process with no say, whatsoever, in any aspect of the curriculum. The teacher is a mere agent who transfers the set material from the higher authorities (the Govt. or Board of Studies) to the students with no consideration of the peculiar situation that he finds himself in. The context in which she teaches the students, their affective states and their needs are altogether ignored by our present system. The teacher who should have been at the top of curriculum framework is at the bottom-most position with no say in its constitution. The examination system is faulty, testing the learners' memory and luck rather than their competence in the various language skills. All these factors have led to a deterioration of the educational system and a serious setback to quality education.

A shift, therefore, needs to be made if our language learning/teaching has to yield positive results. The *Communicative Method in ELT* with its learner-centred focus can help in equipping our students with adequate skills to use language communicatively in different situations. It views language as a creative process with the learner playing a pivotal role. Native language though not completely abandoned becomes a boon rather than a bane in communicating through the target language. All the skills of language are equally acquired to enable the learner to use language effectively. This method takes not only the cognitive and creative aspects of the learner into consideration but also considers his psychological and behavioural aspects. It aims at developing the intrinsic motivation of the students and makes a teacher motivating, stimulating and supervising rather than imposing and thrusting. The shift of emphasis is from teaching to learning with the learner as the focal point. The learner's affective state and his learning needs are adequately catered to. There is an emphasis on acquisition as well practice in language teaching. The emphasis shifts from focusing on the language (i.e. correct grammar and structure) to the functions of language (i.e. what it is used for).

The teacher is the main agent of change and of prime importance in the learner-centred approach. Her roles are varied and manifold and her position in the whole educational system becomes indispensable.

Both the teacher and the learner are considered in every decision-making process of the curriculum. Their views carry weight and their recommendations are incorporated at various levels in the curriculum.

Because of its all-encompassing and multidimensional nature, *The Communicative Method in ELT* is envisaged not only to develop the communicative capacity in our students but also to empower them with the capability 'to learn how to learn' and become self-directive in the long run.

It is with these things in view that I have attempted to make an in-depth assessment of teaching/learning of English at the college level; to mark the limitations and restrictions under which we are presently working and to suggest the remedial measures that need to be taken to come out of our fossilised system in which we have cocooned ourselves and subject ourselves to the changes occurring in the ELT world outside.

The study has taken all the aspects of our teaching/learning situation in view. Chapter 1 deals with the history and evaluation of this rather novel method. It shows how this method evolved, overshadowing all the other methods with its merits. It has come a long way from the 'functional-notional' to the 'interactional task-based' and 'learner-generated' type of teaching. It has changed the focus from the product-oriented to the process-oriented method of teaching/learning.

Chapter 2 deals with the implications that this method has for the teachers and learners in our non-native environment. The heavy demands it makes on the educational system as a whole, and in particular on the teachers and learners, have been discussed in detail.

Chapter 3 deals with the Indian scenario with a special reference to Kashmir. The present curriculum is discussed at length and the drawbacks and shortcomings highlighted. The responses of the teachers and the students from the Kashmir valley regarding various aspects of the curriculum are recorded. It is seen that both the teachers and the students are ready to take up the challenges offered by the Communicative Method. It has been generally accepted that heterogeneity in the proficiency levels of the students, unmanageable classroll, lengthy uninterested literature-oriented courses and faulty teaching methods are the main reasons behind the poor performance of students as far as the use of the language is concerned.

Chapter 4 deals with the actual implementation of the method in our situation. Many suggestions have been put forward that need to be considered. Learner awareness courses, teacher in-service and pre-service training and continuous ongoing evaluation of all the aspects of curriculum (including the teacher, the materials used, the syllabus, the techniques, the method used) are advocated. A teaching model has been proposed for use by teachers.

The study ends on an optimistic note wherein it is believed that the implementation of the Communicative Method is practical. A sincere effort from our experts and the government can set the rails on the tracks and get it going. We all need to pool in our efforts to make the Communicative Method work in our situation and make our education more fruitful and rewarding.

1

The Communicative Methodology in English Language Teaching: Past and Present

Before attempting an analysis of the Communicative Methodology, especially in English language teaching, it would be worthwhile to examine the concept of 'method' itself as 'method' has been interpreted in different ways by different writers. From 1940s onwards various attempts have been made to conceptualize the nature of methods and to explore the relationship between theory and practice within a method.

In the 1960s, Mackey proposed a model for conceptualizing the methods and techniques in language teaching. The basic concepts in Mackey are 'selection,' 'gradation,' 'presentation' and 'repetition.'

All teaching, whether good or bad must include some sort of 'selection', some sort of 'gradation', some sort of 'presentation' and some sort of 'repetition.' Selection, because it is impossible to teach the whole of a field of knowledge; we are forced to select the part of it we wish to teach. Gradation, because it is impossible to teach all of what we have selected at once; we are forced to put something before or after something else. Presentation, because it is impossible to teach without communicating or trying to communicate something to somebody. Repetition, because it is impossible to learn a skill from a single instance; all skill depends on practice.[1]

This is not much different from the model proposed by MacIntosh and Strevens,[2] who use the terms 'limitation' (corresponding to Mackey's selection), 'grading' (corresponding to Mackey's gradations), 'presentation' (corresponding to Mackey's presentation), and 'testing.' Whereas Mackey was primarily concerned with the analysis of textbooks and their underlying principles of organization, Halliday, MacIntosh and Strevens included in their model the entire teaching process.[3] Mackey felt that the method used determined the "success or failure in language learning; for it is ultimately the method that determines the what and how of language instruction."[4]

Mackey's model was limited since it did not address the level of approach, nor did it deal with the actual classroom behaviour of teachers and learners except as these are represented in textbooks. Hence the model failed.

In 1964, Anthony gave a comprehensive model of the theoretical principles and the practices derived from them. He identified three levels of conceptualization and organization which he termed 'approach,' 'method' and 'technique.'

The arrangement is hierarchical. The organization's key is the techniques that carry out a method which is consistent with an approach.... An approach is a set of correlative assumptions dealing with the nature of language teaching and learning. An approach is axiomatic. It describes the nature of the subject matter to be taught.... Method is an overall plan for the orderly presentation of language material, no part of which contradicts, and all of which is based upon the selected approach.... An approach is axiomatic, a method is procedural. Within one approach, there can be many methods.... A technique is implementational—that which actually takes place in a classroom. It is a particular trick, stratagem or contrivance used to accomplish an immediate objective. Technique must be consistent with a method and is, therefore, in harmony with an approach as well.[5]

Though comprehensive, Anthony failed to give sufficient attention to the nature of a method itself. Nothing is said about the role of teachers and learners or about the role of instructional methods.

Richards and Rodgers give a detailed and comprehensive model based on 'approach,' 'design' and 'procedure.'

The first level 'approach' defines those assumptions, beliefs and theories about the nature of language and the nature of language learning that operates in axiomatic constructs or reference point and provides theoretical foundations for what teachers ultimately do with learners in the classroom. The second level 'design' specifies the relationship of theories of language and learning to both the form and function of instructional materials and activities in instructional settings. The third level 'procedure,' comprises classroom techniques and practices that are consequences of particular approach and design.[6]

The 'approach' takes care of the theory of language and theory of language learning; 'design' takes care of the objectives that the method sets out to achieve through the syllabus; the teaching activities that the method advocates are the role of learners, the role of teachers and the role of instructional materials.

Stern defines a method thus:

> A method, however ill-defined it may be is more than a single strategy or a particular technique; it is a 'theory' of language teaching in the T2[7] sense which has resulted from practical and theoretical discussions in a given historical context. It usually implies and sometimes overtly expresses certain objectives and a particular view of language; it makes assumptions about the language learner; and underlying it are certain beliefs about the nature of language learning process. It also expresses a view of language teaching by emphasizing certain aspects of teaching as crucial to successful learning.[8]

Firth and Halliday developed powerful views of language in which meaning and situation were given a prominent place:

> The emphasis now is on the description of language activity as part of the whole complex of events which

together with the participants and relevant objects make up actual situations.[9]

The decade of 1970–1980 saw a reaction against the 'method concept.' Although there was a reaction against the 'method concept,' yet surprisingly several new methods emerged. The Silent Way, a language teaching method (by Gattegno) in the sixties received more recognition in the seventies. Community Language Learning, a method developed in the early sixties by Curran, also found an equally receptive response in the seventies. Also language learning through Suggestopaedia developed by the Bulgarian psychiatrist, Lezanou, was widely discussed.

The period 1970–1980 was marked by four trends: one of the most powerful trends of development was a shift from the concern with methods to the concern with language teaching objectives and the content and curriculum, i.e. the syllabus. In Britain, this was started by Allen, Candlin, Corder, Widdowson, Wilkins and others. In Europe, a novel and influential approach to the language curriculum was made by a group of international scholars who formed the committee of the council for cultural co-operation or the Council of Europe. Their work culminated in the publication of the Threshold Level Syllabuses in English, French, Spanish, German as well as in various writings which proved seminal, e.g. Wilkins,[10] Richterich and Chancerel,[11] Trim[12] and Trim *et al.*[13] Moreover, in Britain and other European countries the concept of languages for special purposes gained momentum. Through needs analysis, attempts were made to meet the varying language needs of the students.

Another important trend of the seventies was a shift of focus from the method concept to a focus on the learner. There was a reaction against the cold mechanical drill techniques of language training of the previous era in favour of cordial atmosphere created in the classroom by the interaction of students among themselves and between the teacher and the students. This is why though there was a revolt against the method concept, the new method which favoured interaction in the classroom and the development of teacher-learner relationship got recognition, e.g. Gattegno's Silent Way,

Curran's Community Language Learning and Lezanou's Suggestopaedia.

There was also a shift from the teaching aspect to an understanding of the learning process itself. This had been voiced in the sixties by Rivers who demanded that "the learner's perceptions, motivation and feelings be taken into account...and that emphasis be shifted from linguistic form to communication in a socio-cultural context."[14]

In the 1970s, Krashen[15] formulated his Monitor-Model theory. This was based on his distinction between the conscious processes of language 'learning' and the less conscious but more important processes of language 'acquisition.' 'Acquisition' referred to the unconscious development of the target language system as a result of using the language for real communication whereas learning is the conscious effort to know the rules of grammar through instruction. Krashen believed that the learned system acts as a Monitor of the output of the acquired system. Krashen postulates nine hypotheses to explain his learning-teaching model.[16]

1. Acquisition and learning hypothesis.
2. The input hypothesis.
3. The monitor hypothesis.
4. The natural order of acquisition hypothesis.
5. The attitude hypothesis.
6. The aptitude hypothesis.
7. The filter hypothesis.
8. The L1 hypothesis.
9. Individual variation in monitor use.

While the first four deal with the language acquisition aspect, the rest deal with the learner himself—his attitudes, his aptitude, his intake capacity and his individual variation in monitor use. The shift from the teaching aspect to the learning process and to the learner himself is therefore evident in Krashen.

The developments from the nineteenth century to our present times are summarized in the chart.[17]

Period	Decade	Main Features
I.	1880-1920	Reform/Direct Method Phonetics
II.	1920-1940	Compromise Method Reading Method BASIC English Modern Foreign Language Study (USA/Canada)
III.	1940-1950	Audiolingual (USA) and Audiovisual (France/Britain) Method FLES Language laboratory Psycholinguistics
	1960-1970	Audiolingual habit theory *vs* cognitive code learning (Carroll 1966) Impact of Chomsky's theory Sociolinguist's Method research Method analysis (Mackey 1965)
IV.	1970-1980	Breakaway from Method Concept — New Method

Curriculum Emphasis	Human Relations Emphasis Research	Language Learning	Silent Way
Speech acts Needs analysis Discourse analysis Language for special purposes Immersion Proficiency levels	Individualization Humanistic techniques	Emphasis on first and second languages child and adult Acquisition/Learning Error analysis Inter-language Studies	Community Language Learning Suggestopaedia etc.

Communicative Approaches

By the early eighties the key concept in language teaching was communication or 'communicative competence.' The term 'communicative competence' was first used by Hymes in deliberate contrast to Chomsky's linguistic competence which was felt as being limited in its concerns since it ignored the use of language in social contexts. Dell Hymes reacted to this by saying, "there are rules of use without which the rules of grammar would be useless." The use of language in social contexts was therefore, *sine qua non* for learning to communicate effectively. Hyme's 'communicative competence' involves:

(a) Whether (and to what degree) something is formally possible.

(b) Whether (and to what degree) something is feasible in virtue of the means of implementation available.

(c) Whether (and to what degree) something is appropriate (adequate, happy, successful) in relation to a context in which it is used and evaluated.

(d) Whether (and to what degree) something is in fact done, actually performed and what its doing entails.[18]

Candlin defines this competence as "the ability to create meanings by exploring the potential inherent in any language for continual modification in response to change, negotiating the value of conventions rather than conforming to established principles."[19]

While Chomsky and Hymes were working in the USA, in Britain, Halliday had already advocated the functional use of language. He writes:

> Linguistics...is concerned...with the description of speech, acts or texts since only through the study of languages in use are all the functions of language and therefore all components of meaning brought into focus.[20]

Halliday described seven basic functions that language performs for children learning their first language.

1. The instrumental functions: using language to get things.

2. The regulatory function: using language to control the behaviour of others.
3. The interactional function: using language to create interaction with others.
4. The personal function: using language to express personal feelings and meanings.
5. The heuristic function: using language to learn and to discover.
6. The imaginative function: using language to create a world of imagination.
7. The representative function: using language to communicate information.[21]

Widdowson believes that the speaker's competence is comprised of both the knowledge of the rules of use and the speaker's grammatical competence. He believes that language learning involves the capacity for the negotiation of meaning achieved only when the learner participates in discourse.

...communicative competence is not a compilation of items in memory but a set of strategies for creative procedures for realizing the values of linguistics elements in contexts of use, an ability to make sense *as a participant in discourse*....[22] (emphasis mine)

For Widdowson the contextualization should be achieved by teaching 'signification' as well as 'value.' Signification is the meaning "which language items have as elements of the language system" and value is the meaning "which they have when they are actually put to use in acts of communication."[23] Widdowson says that 'grammatical' competence remains in a perpetual state of potentiality unless it is realized in communication.[24]

Evelyn Hatch echoes the same notion when she writes, "Language learning even at one-and-two word stages evolves out of learning how to carry on conversations."[25]

This again implies that acquisition of communicative competence in a second language evolves not so much from learning the rules of sentence formation or even producing sentences as from learning by experience the rules of discourse formation by participating actively in them. Allwright draws a logical relationship between linguistic and communicative competence as is clear in the diagram[26] below:

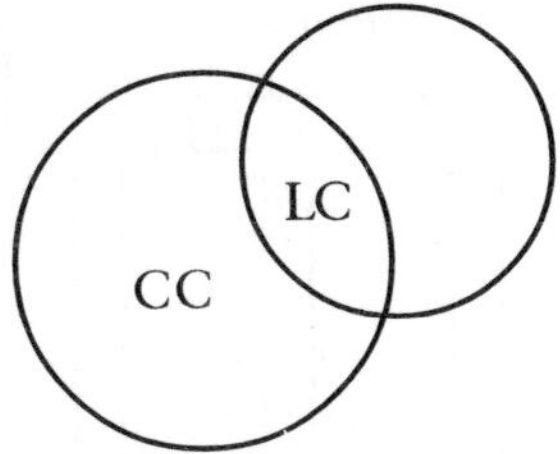

The diagram implies that linguistic competence is only a part of communicative competence. Teaching comprehensively for linguistic competence will leave a large area of communicative competence untouched while teaching for communicative competence will cater to all but a small part of linguistic competence.

A more recent but related analysis of communicative competence is found in Canale and Swain[27] represented by the diagram in which four dimensions of communicative competence are illustrated, sociolinguistic competence, discourse competence and strategic competence are illustrated. Grammatical competence refers to what Chomsky calls 'linguistic competence' and what Hymes intends by the 'formally possible.' It is the domain of grammatical and lexical capacity. Sociolinguistic competence refers to an understanding of the social context in which communication takes place including role relationships, the shared information of the participants and the communicative purpose of their interaction. Textual or discourse competence refers to how meaning is represented in relationship to a discourse or text. Strategic competence refers to the coping strategies that communicators employ to initiate, terminate, maintain, repair and redirect communication. The fact that the grammatical sector is only one of the four parameters of communicative competence shows the comprehensive nature of the communicative act. This is shown in the diagram.[28]

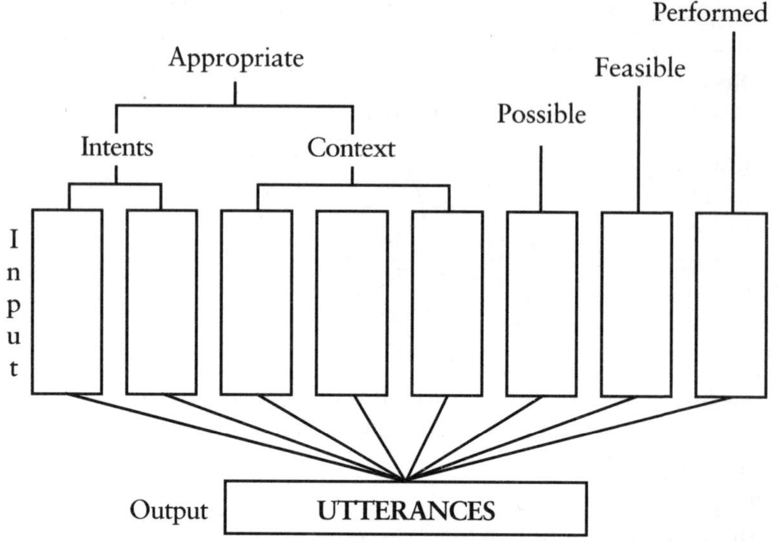

Communication is, therefore, a unique event because it is a combination of many input parameters, none of which can be ignored. The 'possible' parameter would see that the utterance is grammatically correct; the 'feasible' would see it is psycholinguistically implementable; the 'appropriate' would see that it is socio-culturally and contextually appropriate and the 'performed' would see that the utterance[29] is actually in use.

For the utterance to be appropriate the speaker must know "what to say, with whom, when and where."[30] Halliday talks of the "textual function" of language as having to do with "making links with itself and with features of the situation in which it is used."[31] Bachman feels that "the notion of pragmatic competence...includes elocutionary competence, or the knowledge of the pragmatic conventions for performing acceptable language functions and sociolinguistic conventions for performing language functions approximately in a given context."[32] Austin[33] calls the literal meaning of an utterance as the locutionary force and the contextual meaning that the utterance takes in use as the ilocutionary force. Allan feels, "the curriculum should be based both on a formal and functional analysis and at the same time offer opportunities for experiential participation in real life communication which by its very nature is non-analytical.[34]

Candlin feels that there must be an adequate pedagogical grammar which "cannot be limited to sentences but must act as interpreter of discourse, and as such its requirements are more onerous than existing linguistic grammar. It must deal not only with the grammaticality and acceptability of sentences but the pragmatics of language use."[35]

The history of language teaching reveals that communication has always been the goal of language courses, though orientations and methodology have been changed over the years.[36] The communicative method developed its framework (syllabus) from within notional syllabuses. For the first time language syllabus was "based on an analysis of the needs of the learners."[37] Wilkins analysed the communicative meanings that a language learner needs to understand and express, rather than describe "the core of language through traditional concepts of grammar and vocabulary, it (a notional syllabus) attempts to demonstrate the systems of meanings that lay behind the communicative uses of language."[38] He described two types of meanings—notional categories (concepts such as time, sequence, quantity, location and frequency) and categories of communicative function (requests, denials, offers, complaints). Communication is, therefore, a three-dimensional activity involving 'meanings,' 'structures' and the resulting 'utterances.' The notional approach is definitely different from the earlier approaches. Here, the form of the language is subservient to the meanings that the learner conveys through the target language. The materials based on the notional syllabus are, therefore, linguistically heterogeneous. Widdowson, however, criticized this approach on the grounds that it did not account for how learners participated in discourse. He writes:

> What such a syllabus does not do or has not done to date (an important proviso)—is to present language as discourse and since it does not, it cannot possibly in its present form account for communicative competence—because communicative competence is not a compilation of items

in memory but a set of strategies for creative procedures for realizing the value of linguistic elements in contexts of use....[39]

The council of Europe, however, incorporated its semantic/ communicative analysis into a set of specifications for a first level communicative language syllabus.

The communicative method was a revolt against the structuralist approach to language description as well as the behaviourist theory of language learning which had characterized teaching method like Audiolingualism (in America) and the Situational Language Teaching (in Britain). Speech was given the first priority as Rivers writes: "Language is speech, not writing.... A language is a set of habits.... Teach the language not about the language."[40]

Since Audiolingualism was based on the behaviourist theory, it emphasized reinforcement as a vital element in the learning process. Language mastering was represented as acquiring a set of appropriate language stimulus-response chains. Since structure is important and unique in a language, early practice should focus on mastery of phonological and grammatical structures rather than on mastery of vocabulary.

The British theoreticians, however had a different focus to their version of structuralism—the notion of 'situation.' As Pittman remarks:

> Our principal classroom activity in the teaching of English structure will be the oral practice of structures. This oral practice of controlled sentence patterns should be given in situations designed to give the greatest amount of practice in English speech to the pupils.[41]

The theory that knowledge of structures must be linked to situations gave situational language teaching[42] one of its distinctive features. Both Firth and Halliday gave meaning, context and situation a prominent place in language teaching.[43]

The main features of situational language teaching were that spoken form is of prime importance, and that language should be taught situationally. The target language should be the medium of instruction and grammar should be taught in a graded manner with simple forms first and complex ones later.

The need to present language in a context with the help of gestures and actions can be traced back to the nineteenth century French linguist Glouin, who used situations and sequences of related actions (the famous 'gouins' series) as ways of organizing and presenting oral language. Likewise, the primacy of speech over writing can again be traced back to the nineteenth century Reform Movement when the International Phonetic Association was founded (in 1886). The Reform Movement was an interest in developing principles for language teaching out of naturalistic principles of language learning such as seen in first language acquisition. This led to what had been termed Natural Methods[44] and ultimately to the development of the Direct Method. The Direct Method advocated extensive use of the target language in the classroom and the inductive way of teaching grammar. Speech was of first priority with emphasis on correct pronunciation and oral communication skills.

The Direct Method was a revolt against the Grammar-Translation Method which had dominated language teaching from 1840s to 1940s. It approached language first through detailed analysis of its grammar rules and second through translation into the mother tongue. As Stern writes:

The first language is maintained as the reference system in the acquisition of the second language.[45]

No attention is paid to speech, accuracy is emphasized, grammar is taught deductively and most important the student's native language is the medium of instruction.

One major misleading generalization that follows the Grammar-Translation Method (or any product-oriented method) is the transfer of knowledge from rules to practice. It is generally believed that it is imperative to teach the grammar rules and the language use will automatically follow. Such a knowledge "provides the basis for actual use of language by the speaker-hearer."[46] The assumption being that once the basis is provided then the learner will have no difficulty in dealing with actual language use, i.e., once 'competence' is acquired 'performance' will follow. This has proved to be a fallacy. Newman cites the examples of a person:

> Who knows perfectly the structures that the linguist teaches (yet), cannot know the way to get his cigarette lit by a stranger when he has no matches. He has to walk up to him and say one of the utterances, "so you have a lighter, got a match." Not one of the equally well-formed questions, "Do you have illumination? or Do you have fire? or Are you matches owner?"[47]

The assumption is that form and meaning are in one-to-one relationship with each other. The truth, however, is that whereas the sentence structure may be stable or straightforward, its communicative function is variable and depends upon specific situations and social factors. A form may function in many ways and the meaning of a sentence may change according to the way it is said and when. From a communicative point of view using language well is not a simple question of grammaticality but one of overall 'appropriacy,' 'acceptability' and 'feasibility.'

The communicative method basis language teaching is the use of language in communication. It is sometimes said that a structural approach when it is orally based with plenty of classroom activity succeeds in using language communicatively. It does not. It is important not to confuse plenty of "student talk" with learning to communicate. They are not synonyms. Typically, there is a great deal of doings, learners reading passages, composing sentences, busy practising the four skills but all this is done to consolidate their knowledge of language rules not to put them into communication. No matter how many grammatical forms may appear in a structural dialogue, the focus is always a structural one. No account is offered of how a sentence takes on meaning from its relation to surrounding utterances and non-linguistic factors. The result of purely structural practice is the ability to produce a range of 'usage'[48] but not the ability to 'use' forms appropriately. He further adds, "A knowledge of use must of necessity, include a knowledge of usage but the reverse is not the case."[49] The teaching of usage does not guarantee a knowledge of use whereas the teaching of use does seem to guarantee the knowledge of usage. It seems desirable therefore, to design language teaching courses with reference to use. A need has been felt to shift from the grammatical syllabus to a communicative syllabus for widening the scope of language context beyond grammatical structures, lexis and pronunciation to functions, notions, settings and so on:

> Learning, however, is more than just a matter of presenting language items or skills and strategies. In other words, it is not just the context of what is learnt that is important but also the activity through which it is learnt.[50]

The communicative method makes sure that the interactions which take place in the classroom are replications of or necessary prerequisites for a communicative operation. The focus changes from the sentence production of isolated utterances to the fluent selection of appropriate utterances in communication. The learner is concerned with 'using' language rather than with 'usage.' In order to do this, the learner takes on roles and interacts with other learners who also take up roles. In such a communicative practice there is no control on the response. The student has free choice of answer and the extension of selection is his own opinion. Brumfit advocates the use of small groups in language classrooms:

> Small groups provide greater intensity of involvement so that the quality of language practice is increased, and opportunities for feedback and monitoring also, given adequate guidance and preparation by the teacher.... Experience also suggests that placing student in small groups assists individualisation....[51]

Harmer endorses this view on grounds that it gives students opportunities "to use language to communicate with each other.... Students will be teaching and learning in the group exhibiting a degree of self-reliance that simply is not possible when the teacher is acting as a controller."[52]

A wide range of activities have been proposed for use in the classroom. They are mostly problem-solving activities and require the use of such communicative processes as information sharing, negotiation of meaning and interaction. Rivers talks of 'skill getting' and 'skill using' activities. She feels that the 'skill getting' activities rarely pass beyond 'pseudo-communication' while the 'skill using' activities help the students to "leap into autonomy," as shown in the figure[53] below (taken from Rivers):

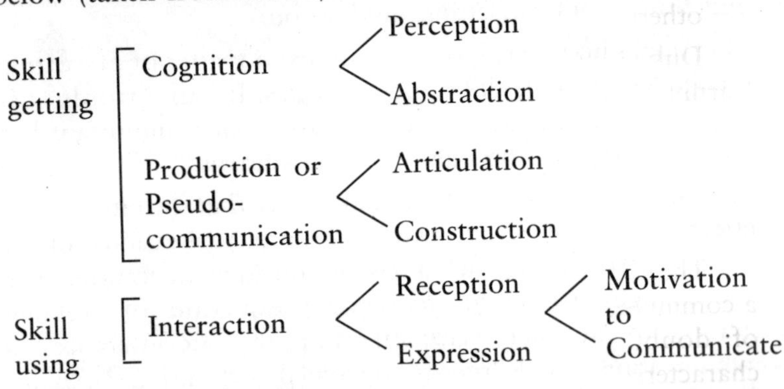

The aim is to proceed from controlled drills to autonomous interactions or as Brumfit[54] puts it from 'accuracy' to 'fluency.' 'Fluency' does not only mean emphasis on stress and intonation (though these are equally essential for effective communication) but also enough opportunities for conversation/discussion in informed pairs/groups to give learners ability to exploit their limited knowledge of the language in natural interactional situations. This must exist with the provision for teaching accuracy. By 'accuracy' is meant the provision for everything which enables a learner to learn language consciously—the model underlying most teaching. It includes the presentation of controlled samples of the language together with guidance as to the system which underlies them. The 'fluency' element needs to be properly integrated with 'accuracy.' These can be attempted in various ways. As Johnson writes:

> These attempts may take many forms. Wright (1976) achieves it by showing out-of-focus slides which the students attempt to identify. Byrne (1978) provides incomplete plans and diagrams which students have to complete by asking for information. Allwright (1977) places a screen

between students and gets one to place objects in a certain pattern; this pattern is then communicated to students behind the screen. Geddes and Sturtridge (1979) develop 'jig-saw' listening in which students listen to different taped materials and then communicate their content to others in the class. Most of these techniques operate by providing information to some and withholding it from others.[55]

Dubin and Olshtain[56] use the term 'workouts' for language learning and language using activities which enhance both the acquisition process and the communication output process. Each workout type focuses on a special aspect of language use yet together they aim at helping the learner become a more effective language user.

The range of exercise types and activities compatible with a communicative approach are unlimited, however, the element of doubt and lack of information or information gap characterizes them all. For communication to take place, some gaps must be provided so that a need is felt to bridge those information gaps. There must be a reason to communicate—a demand to communicate. Gaps create those demands. This concept of information gaps is central to the whole area of communicative teaching and one of the main jobs for the teacher can be seen as setting up situations where information gaps exist and also motivating the students to bridge them in appropriate ways.

Allwright believes, "If the language teacher's management activities are directed exclusively at invoking the learners in solving communication problems in the target language then language will take care of itself...."[57]

A crucial characteristic of communication is that the participants have choice both in terms of what they will say and how they will say it. The choice which is open for the speaker means that there is always a doubt in the listener's mind about what is to come next. This element of doubt is central to real communication in the classroom.

Another crucial element in communicative teaching is the Task dependency Principle.[58] Task dependency is created by making, say, task 3, dependent on task 2, task 4, dependent on task 3 and so on. This Task dependency makes listening, reading and writing purposeful by making it mandatory for the learner to utilize the information in one task to perform another task.

Harmer feels that:

> Whatever activity the students are involved in, if it is to be genuinely communicative and if it is really promoting language use, the students *should have a reason* to communicate (emphasis mine). If they want to be involved in communication then that communication should have some kind of communicative purpose, in other words they should be using language in some way to achieve an objective, and this objective (or purpose) should be the most important part of the communication.[59]

The materials used in a communicative language class may vary from the use of textbooks to task-based materials like role plays, simulations and task based communicative activities to 'Realia' or the use of 'authentic'—'from-life' materials in the classroom.

The aim is to develop communicative competence in our students. There is no single universally accepted model for communicative language teaching. Littlewood states, "one of the most characteristic features of communicative language teaching is that it pays systematic attention to functional as well as structural aspects of language."[60] He emphasizes practice as a way of developing communicative skills which has both a cognitive and a behavioural aspect. The cognitive aspect involves the grammatical rules, vocabulary and social conventions governing speech while the behavioural aspect involves real use of these rules in everyday speech. "This occurs mainly through practice in converting plans into performance."[61]

Howatt distinguishes between a 'strong' and a 'weak' version of communicative language teaching. He writes:

> There is, in a sense, a 'strong' version of the communicative

approach and a 'weak' version. The 'weak' version which has become more or less standard practice in the last ten years, stresses the importance of providing learners with opportunities to use their English for communicative purposes and characteristically attempt to integrate such activities into a wider program of language teaching.... The 'strong' version of communicative teaching, on the other hand, advances the claim that language is acquired through communication so that it is not merely a question of activating an existing but inert knowledge of the language but of stimulating the development of the language system itself. If the former could be described as 'learning to use' English the latter entails 'using English to learn it.'[62]

Yalden[63] describes the major current communicative trends in language teaching. Richards and Rodgers[64] modify Yalden's classification of communicative syllabus types with reference source to each model.

Type	Reference
1. Structures plus functions	Wilkins (1976)
2. Functional spiral around a structural core	Brumfit (1980)
3. Structural, functional, instrumental	Allen (1980)
4. Functional	Jupp and Holdin (1975)
5. Notional	Wilkins (1976)
6. Interactional	Widdowson (1979)
7. Task-based	Prabhu (1983)
8. Learner-generated	Candlin (1976) Heuner-Stanchina and Riley (1978)

There has been a recent trend (in ELT) of shifting from the structural, functional and notional syllabuses to the interactional, task-based and learner-generated syllabuses. The current interest is in framing process-oriented rather than product-oriented syllabuses. One such syllabus has been proposed by Breen where he suggests that an alternative to the listing of linguistic content be made with focus upon the process rather than predetermined end. "...all indicate *priority of process over content.*"[65] (emphasis mine).

What Breen is suggesting is that with communication at the centre of the curriculum, the goal of that curriculum and the means which develop this capability begin to merge; the syllabus must take account of both the ends and the means.

Long's task-based approach is based on a related assumption that the specific nature of the task and the content on which it is based are unimportant as long as learners are productively engaged in performing a task.[66]

N.S. Prabhu, the former British Council English Studies Officer in Madras, feels that:

> The only form of syllabus which is compatible with and can support comunicational teaching seems to be a purely procedural one—which lists in more or less detail, the types of tasks to be attempted in the classroom and suggests an order of complexity for tasks of the same kind.[67]

Prabhu started a five-year-project of exploratory teaching which helped to articulate the view that the development of competence in a second language requires not systematization of language inputs or maximization of planned practice but rather the creation of conditions in which learners engage in an effort to cope with communication. The pedagogical perception behind the project is that language ability develops in direct relation to communicational effort. Teaching should create opportunities for the students to use language rather than stress grammar rules.

The activity that the learner engages in is called 'task.' A 'task' consists of a 'pre-task,' a 'task-cycle' and a 'language-focus phase.' The 'pre-task' introduces learners to the topic and the task in which the teacher highlights the useful words and phases. In the 'task-cycle' phases the learners do the task in pairs and small groups to develop fluency. They finally exchange their report or present it to the class and compare results. In the 'language-focus phase' students examine and discuss specific features of the text and then take part in teacher-conducted practice of new words, phrases and patterns. "The 'pre-task' and the task pattern divides a lesson desirably into an initial period of whole-class activity, teacher direction and oral interaction and a later period of sustained self-dependent effort by learners."[68]

David Nunan defines task as:

> A piece of classroom work which involves learners in comprehending, manipulating, producing or interacting in the target language while their attention is principally focused on meaning rather than form.[69]

Nunan distinguishes between 'product-oriented' tasks and 'process-oriented' tasks. The 'product-oriented' tasks specify "what learners will be able to do as a result of instruction and process-oriented tasks specify the activities to be undertaken during instruction."[70] The emphasis is on communicating meaning rather than on concentrating on form. Long and Crookes found that "increasing the number of referential over display questions and developing what they call 'two-way tasks' led to an increase in the amount of genuine communicative language used in the classroom and also to higher scores on tests of content."[71]

The communicative method seems to be rapidly shifting towards total learner-centredness and learner-autonomy.

Leo Van Lier voices his three fundamental principles of awareness, autonomy and authenticity (AAA). The learner is encouraged to become an autonomous self-regulated person. 'Awareness' is described as the process of paying attention to new experiences and relating them to existing knowledge. "'Autonomy' has to do with choice and responsibility with the learners' initiative in making decisions about what is to be learnt. 'Authenticity' is related to action that is instrinsically motivated when a learner has a genuine desire to learn rather then being compelled by some external force to do so. The close relationship between these concepts is evident in that authenticity is at the same time the result and the origin of awareness and autonomy."[72]

Rejecting the input/output model of language acquisition, Van Lier advances a richer conceptualization of the educational process, granting a more powerful role to the learner's cognitive effort in processing what he or she chooses to learn. Thus, receptivity on the learners' part is viewed as crucial in facilitating engagement with language, which in conjunction with investment results in successful intake.

Van Lier reaffirms the central role of instrinsic motivation in fostering self-regulation and commitment to the learner, as opposed to external inducement which discourages and inhibits autonomy.

A multilayered teaching strategy is advocated consisting of tasks and activities that are partly planned, partly improvised and that aid moment-to-moment decision-making. Tasks and activities that carefully balance the demands between learning, content and action and build in flexibility are considered more useful; on the other hand, prescribed textbooks and materials have a less prominent place in an AAA curriculum.

A similar kind of a curriculum was proposed by David Nunan in 1988 in his book *The Learner-Centred Curriculum.*[73] He proposed that learners themselves be taken as the central reference point for decision-making regarding both the content and the form of language teaching and that this goal should be realized interactively by a process of consultation and negotiation between the participants in the learning situation. Learners' education thus constitutes a key factor in Nunan's view of language teaching, learners' participation in goal-setting and in the selection of methodology depending crucially on the development of learners' understanding of language and of language learning. The learners should have sufficient understanding of language learning to understand the purpose of pedagogical choices; they should be able to formulate their own learning objectives; they should be able to make use of appropriate learning strategies; they should be able to monitor their use of these strategies; they should be able to self-assess or monitor their own learning. The concern with the development of learner-autonomy has given rise to research into the means of acquiring these skills in the learners so that they operate in an informed and self-directive manner. Thus 'learner-training' becomes a crucial component of the Autonomous Learner-Centred Approach.

Ian Tudor in his book *Learner-Centredness as Language Education* sees learner-centred learning as an open-ended endeavour in which the socio-cultural aspects of the learners' identity are considered as much as the individual aspects of his identity. The book recommends a participatory and negotiative approach in all decision-making issues. This implies that learners are called upon to play a more active role in decision-making than in the case of traditional, teacher-driven approaches. The book rests on the belief, "...education, in whatever field, should seek to provide students not only with discrete knowledge and skills but also with the capacity to operate in an informed and self-directive manner.... In this perspective, education is seen as a means of empowerment."[74]

Thus, we see that the Communicative Method has gone a long way from the functional, notional, to the interactional, task-based and finally the autonomous learner-generated curriculum design. However all have some features in common which make them markedly different from the traditional structural one. The main distinguishing features can be summarized as follows:

Communicative Syllabus Design	Structural Syllabus Design
1. From the very beginning the main emphasis is on the use of the language in communicative situations.	1. From the very beginning main emphasis is on internalizing the rules of grammar.
2. Grammar is taught inductively.	2. Grammar is taught deductively.
3. The contents are based cyclically, i.e., a course is designed to expand the learners' semantic	3. The contents are based in a linear manner with variation in the steepness of the grading and the

Communicative Syllabus Design	Structural Syllabus Design
repertoire progressively. At the lowest level he can express them only in the simplest manner. By the time he reaches the most advanced levels of learning, he has at his disposal a range of expressions capable of communicating the same notions with far greater subtlety and skill.	specification of the end objective.
4. The contents of learning are based on a multitude of conditions, i.e., conditions related to the situation, the students and their needs. A fixed relation is not possible.	4. The contents of learning are not specially dependent on the conditions of learning. A fixed relation is adapted even if the conditions of learning change.
5. Course design is a negotiated process. There is no single factor which has an outright determining influence on the content of the course. The ESP learning situation and the target situation will both influence the nature of the syllabus, materials, methodology and evaluation procedures. Each of these components will influence and be influenced by the other.	5. Course design is a settled process. No factor related to the learners or the situation or the needs is taken into account.
6. Course design is a dynamic process. It changes with the needs and resources	6. Course design is a static process and does not change even if the needs

Communicative Syllabus Design	Structural Syllabus Design
which vary with time. The course design needs to be built in feedback channels to enable the course to respond to developments. The syllabus takes account of both means and ends and must address both content and process.	and resources change. The syllabus takes account of only the end and not the means, i.e. it addresses the content and not the process.
7. The materials used are primarily based on the interests and needs of the learners, taking their motivational level into account.	7. The materials used are not to the interest and needs of the students. Moreover, their motivational level is not taken into account.
8. Materials necessarily include interesting texts and enjoyable activities which provide the learners with opportunities to use their existing knowledge and skills.	8. The texts are usually monotonous and boring. They are irrelevant to the learners.
9. Conscious learning is only a part of the method which encourages language acquisition through a large amount of input and a significant emphasis on the use of language in communicative activities.	9. Learning is stressed more than acquisition.
10. Critical self-awareness is aimed at.	10. No such awareness is developed.
11. Evaluation is carried on	11. Evaluation is carried on

Communicative Syllabus Design	Structural Syllabus Design
alongside the teaching learning process by the teachers and the learners.	at the end by the teachers alone.
12. Information by and from learners will be built into every phase of the curriculum process.	12. No such collaborative effort is possible.
13. Any element within the curriculum may be evaluated. At the planning stage, needs analysis techniques and procedures may be evaluated, while during implementation, materials learning activities, learning arrangements, teacher performance and learners achievement may be evaluated.	13. Only the structural-content is evaluated.

With these new dimensions the communication method is bound to be radically different from the traditional methods. Not only will the syllabus undergo a change but the materials used, the techniques used in the classroom and above all the role of the teacher will change drastically. All these will have an impact on the overall teaching situation. Richards and Rogers summarize the problem that CLT poses thus:

> The communicative approach raised important issues for teacher training, materials development and testing and evaluation. Questions that have been raised include whether a communicative approach can be applied at all levels in a teaching programme, whether it requires existing grammar-based syllabus to be abandoned or merely revised, how much an approach can be evaluated, how suitable it is for non-native teachers and how it can be adopted in situations

where students must continue to take grammar-based texts.[75]

Whether these problems can be solved; whether the changes that the communicative method implies can be assimilated and accommodated in our present situation remains to be seen and it is to this point that we will turn in the chapter that follows.

REFERENCES

1. W.F. Mackey. *Language Teaching Analysis*. London: Longman, 1965, 157.
2. M.A.K. Halliday, A. MacIntosh and P. Strevens. *The Linguistic Science and Language Teaching*. London: Longman, 1964.
3. Mackey called his model 'Method Analysis' while Halliday, MacIntosh and Strevens called it 'Methodics.'
4. W.F. Mackey. *Language Teaching Analysis*. 1965, 138.
5. E.M. Anthony. 'Approach, Method and Technique,' *English Language Teaching*, 1963, 17:63-7.
6. J.C. Richards and T.S. Rodgers. *Approaches and Methods in Language Teaching*. Cambridge: Cambridge University Press, 1986, 17.
7. Stern uses the word theory in context. First in its widest sense (T1) to refer to the systematic study of thought related to a topic or activity, e.g. art, music or education. In this sense, a theory offers a system of thought, a method of analysis or synthesis. In its second sense it is possible to subsume different schools of thought or theories (T2) each with their own assumptions, postulates, principles, models and concepts. Lastly, in the natural and human sciences the concept of theory is employed in a more rigorous third sense (T3) as a hypothesis or set of hypotheses that have been verified by observation or experiment whose main function is to explain their subject matter.
8. H.H. Stern. *Fundamental Concept of Language Teaching*. Oxford: Oxford University Press, 1983, 453.
9. M.A.K. Halliday, K. MacIntosh and P. Strevens. *The Linguistic Science and Language Teaching*, 38.
10. D.A. Wilkins. *Notional Syllabuses*. London: Oxford University Press, 1976.
11. R. Richterich and J.L. Chancerel. *Identifying the Needs of Adults Learning a Foreign Language*. Strasbourg, Council of Europe: Pergamon Press, 1980.
12. J.L.M. Trim. *Developing a Unit/Credit Scheme of Adult Language Learning*. Oxford: Pergamon Press, 1980.
13. J.L.M. Trim *et al*. *Systems Development in Adults Language Learning: A European Unit/Credit System for Modern Language Learning by Adults*. Oxford: Pergamon Press, 1980.

14. W.M. Rivers. *The Psychologist and the Foreign Language Teacher.* Chicago and London: University of Chicago Press, 1964, 163.
15. S.D. Krashen. *Second Language Acquisition and Second Language Learning.* Oxford: Pergamon, 1981.
16. Quoted in Mohamad Aslam. *Developing a Learner-Centered ELT Curriculum in India: Trends and Issues.* Bareilly: Prakash Book Depot, 1997, 109-110.
17. H.H. Stern. *Fundamental Concepts of Language Teaching,* 113.
18. D. Hymes. 'On Communicative Competence' in J.B. Pride and J. Holmes (eds.). *Socio-linguistic: Selected Readings.* Harmondsworth: Penguin Books, 1972, 278.
19. C.N. Candlin. 'Explaining Communicative Competence Limits of Testability' in C.W. Stanfield. *Towards Communicative Competence Testing: Proceedings of the Second TEFL Invitational Conference.* Prinception, NJ: Educational Testing Service. 1986, 40.
20. M.A.K. Halliday. 'Language Structure and Language Functions' in John Lyons (ed.). *New Horizons in Linguistics.* London: Penguin, 1970, 145.
21. M.A.K. Halliday. *Learning How to Mean.* Edward Arnold: London, 1975, 11-17.
22. H.G. Widdowson. *Explanations in Applied Linguistics.* Oxford: Oxford University Press, 1979, 248.
23. H.G. Widdowson. 'The Teaching of English as Communication' in L.J. Brumfit and R. Johnson (eds.). *The Communicative Approach to Language Teaching.* Oxford: Oxford University Press, 1979, 118.
24. *Ibid* - 50. Our present system teaches 'signification' and not 'value' and that is why it is inadequate for the teaching of English as communication.
25. Quoted in R.W. Blair (ed.). *Innovative Approach to Language Teaching.* USA: Newzburry House Publishers, 1982, 193.
26. Richard Allwright. 'Language Learning Through Communication' in Brumfit & Johnson (eds.). 1979, 168.
27. M. Canale and M. Swain. 'Theoretical Bases of Communicative Approaches to Second Language Teaching and Testing.' *Applied Linguistics,* 91, 1980, 1-47.
28. From Keith Johnson. *Communicative Syllabus Design and Methodology.* Oxford: Pergamon Press, 1982, 203.
29. Utterance is different from a sentence in that while the sentence refers to well-formed strings output from the grammar the former refers to the units of discourse characterized by their use value in communication. (Brumfit and Johnson, 1979, 79).
30. D. Hymes. 'On Communicative Competence.' in J.B. Pride and J. Holmes (eds.). 1972, 14.
31. M.A.K. Halliday. 'Language Structure and Language Function' in Lyons (ed.). *New Horizons in Linguistics.* Penguin book, 1970, 143.

32. L.F. Bachman. *Fundamental Considerations in Language Testing*. Oxford: Oxford University Press, 1990, 90.
33. Quoted in John Munby. *Communicative Syllabus Design*. 1978.
34. Quoted in H.H. Stern. *Fundamental Concepts of Language Teaching*. 262.
35. C.N. Candlin. 'The Status of Pedagogical Grammars' in C.J. Brumfit and R. Johnson (ed.). *The Communicative Approach to Language Teaching*. Oxford: Oxford University Press, 1979, 75.
36. D.A. Wilkins. 'Geometrical Situational and Notional Syllabuses' in Brumfit & Johnson (eds.). 1979, 82-90.
37. D.A. Wilkins. *Notional Syllabuses*. London: Oxford University Press, 1976, 55.
38. J.C. Richards & T.S. Rodgers. *Approaches and Methods in Language Teaching*. 1986, 65.
39. H.G. Widdowson. *Explorations in Applied Linguistics*. Oxford: Oxford University Press. 1979, 248.
40. W.M. Rivers. *The Psychologist and the Foreign Language Teacher*. Chicago University of Chicago Press, 1964, 5.
41. G. Pittman. *Teaching Situational English*. London: Evans. 1963, 179.
42. This was also called "*The Oral Approach*."
43. See page 8 for details.
44. Natural Method was associated with L. Sauveur (1826-1907) who opened a school in Boston in the late 1860s and his method soon became referred to as the Natural Method.
45. H.H. Stern. *Fundamental Concepts of Language Teaching*. 1983, 455.
46. N. Chomsky. *Aspects of the Theory of Syntax*. Cambridge: MIT Press, 1965, 9.
47. L. Newmark. 'How not to Interfere with Language Learning' in Brumfit and Johnson (eds.). 1979, 161.
48. Widdowson makes a distinction between 'usage' (structure, grammar or what Chomsky calls competence) and 'use' (using language in communication).
49. H.G. Widdowson. *Teaching Language as Communication*. Oxford: Oxford University Press, 1978, 18.
50. Tom Hutchinson and Alan Waters. *English for Specific Purposes*. Cambridge: Cambridge University Press, 1987, 92.
51. C. Brumfit. *Communicative Methodology in Language Teaching: The Roles of Fluency and Accuracy*. Cambridge: Cambridge University Press, 1984, 778.
52. Jeremy Harmer. *The Practice of English Language Teaching*. Longman Series. 1983, 44.

53. W.M. Rivers. *Communicating Naturally in Second Language: Theory and Practice in Language Teaching*. Chicago: The University of Chicago Press, 1983, 43.

54. C.J. Brumfit. 1984, 119-136.

55. K. Johnson. *Communicative Syllabus Design and Methodology*. Oxford: Pergamon Press, 1982, 151.

56. Fraida Dubin and Elite Olshtain. *Course Design*. Cambridge: Cambridge University Press, 1986, 95.

57. R.L. Allwright. '*Language Learning Through Communication Practice*.' ELT Documents 76, 3: 2-14.

58. K. Johnson and K. Morrow (eds.). *Communication in the Classroom*. London: Longman, 83-99.

59. Jeremy Harmer. *The Practice of English Language Teaching*. Longman Series. 1983, 44.

60. W. Littlewood. *Communicative Language Teaching: An Introduction*. Cambridge: Cambridge University Press, 1981, 1.

61. W. Littlewood. *Foreign and Second Language Learning: Language Acquisition Research and its Implications for the Classroom*. Cambridge: Cambridge University Press, 1984, 74.

62. A.P.R. Howatt. *A History of English Language Teaching*. Oxford: Oxford University Press, 1984, 279.

63. J. Yalden. *The Communicative Syllabus: Evolution, Design and Implementation*. Oxford: Pergamon Press, 1983.

64. J.C. Richards and T.S. Rogers. *Approaches and Methods in Language Teaching*. 74.

65. Breen 1984, 52-3.

66. This is an alternative to the comprehensible input hypothesis of Krashen. It believes in the comprehensible output hypothesis (of Swain, 1985) which stresses the importance of giving learners opportunities for practising the target language.

67. N.S. Prabhu. 'Procedural Syllabuses.' Paper read at the *RELC Seminar*. Singapore, 1983, 4.

68. N.S. Prabhu. *Second Language Pedagogy*. Oxford: Oxford University Press, 1987, 55.

69. David Nunan. *Designing Tasks for the Communicative Classroom*. Cambridge: Cambridge University Press, 1989, 10.

70. David Nunan. 1989, 61.

71. Quoted in R.K. Johnson. *The Second Language Curriculum*. Cambridge: Cambridge University Press, 1989, 185.

72. Leo Van Lier. 'Interaction in the Language Curriculum: Awareness, Autonomy and Authenticity' in *ELT Journal* Vol. 52/2 April 1998. Oxford University Press, 1998, 166.

73. David Nunan. *The Learner-Centred Curriculum*. Cambridge: Cambridge University Press, 1988.
74. Ian Tudor. *Learner-Centredness as Language Education*. Cambridge University Press, 1996 (xi).
75. J.C. Richards and T.S. Rodgers. *Approaches and Methods in Language Teaching*, 1986, 83.

2

Communicative Method in Teaching English for Non-Native Environments

The Communicative Method makes heavy demands on the learners as well as on the teachers. In fact, it has an impact on the system as a whole. It cannot be considered in isolation but demands an awareness and assessment of what the existing situation is and what activities would be needed to improve or change it in order to make it useful to the learners in a given community. Jernudd and Gupta stress this point thus:

> The planner must investigate the existing setting to ascertain what problems are as viewed both by persons who will execute the plan and by persons who will be targets of the plan. It is important for him to know what constraints, tendencies and rationalization the existing social cultural and economic parameters offer.[1]

Mackey places language learning into its socio-political context. He identifies five major variables: M (methods and materials, e.g. textbook, tapes and films), T (what the teacher does), I (instruction, what the learner gets), S (socio-linguistic and socio-cultural influences of the environment) and L (what the learner does). Mackey's conceptual framework as illustrated in the diagram[2] below indicates how the teaching variables (the MTI triangle in the diagram) as well as the learning variables (the ISL triangle) are dependent upon political social and educational factors.

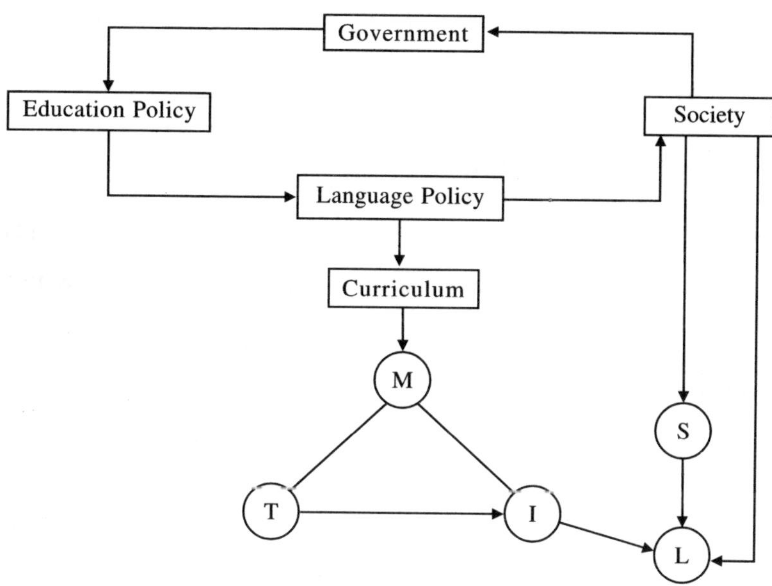

This leads us to the interrelation of the curriculum with the educational policy and society on the one hand and with methodology on the other. Candlin believes that our syllabus "rather than being an ordered sequence of selected...items of content...reveals itself as a window on a particular set of social, education, moral and subject matter values. Syllabuses seen in this perspective stand then, for particular ideologies."[3] As projection of educational policy then, a curriculum and the different syllabuses within it will conform to varying ideological decisions about the purpose and nature of education as a whole. It is for this reason that Widdowson believes:

> ...that pedagogy, no matter how well supported by theories of learning, must come to terms with local educational attitudes and policies. These are bound to constrain what can be done in syllabus design and in classroom methodology.[4]

Widdowson believes, "The design of a syllabus therefore needs to take into account both the prevailing educational attitudes of a particular community and current thinking to the extent that it is deemed to be well informed about the conditions that promote learning in general.... The essential point is that one cannot devise a pedagogically desirable syllabus...without regard to particular educational contexts."[5]

Allen is of the view, "...a particular conceptual or philosophical orientation can have a far-reaching effect on what takes place in the classroom."[6]

Curriculum

It follows that curriculum is a broad term which incorporates a "whole complex of philosophical, social and administrative factors which contribute to the planning of an educational programme. Syllabus on the other hand, refers to that subpart of curriculum which is concerned with a specification of what units will be taught (as distinct from how they will be taught which is a matter of methodology)."[7]

Clark[8] talks of three educational value systems, namely 'Classical Humanism,' 'Reconstructionism' and 'Progressivism' which have their effect on curriculum design, the foreign language curriculum and policies for curriculum renewal.

'Classical Humanism' gives rise to a content-driven curriculum (like our existing syllabuses) in which the subject-matter is analysed into elements of knowledge which are then sequenced from simple to complex. In terms of educational policy it adopts a policy in which change is to be brought about slowly.

'Reconstructionism' gives rise to a goal-driven curriculum in which the content is derived from an analysis of the learners' objective needs. In terms of educational policy it adopts a 'top-down' policy in which a committee of government-appointed experts comes to some consensus on what should be done next and imposes the desired curriculum upon educational institutions which later adopt it.

'Progressivism' gives rise to a process-driven curriculum in which learners negotiate goals, content and methods and impose their own order on what is learnt. It adopts a 'bottom-up' policy in which the teachers together with the learners decide what is to be done next.

A communicative curriculum draws from three major areas: a view of the nature of language as seen by the field of sociolinguistics, a cognitively based view of language learning and a humanistic approach in education. These theoretical views which influence the goals of a communicative curriculum are shown in the diagram.[9]

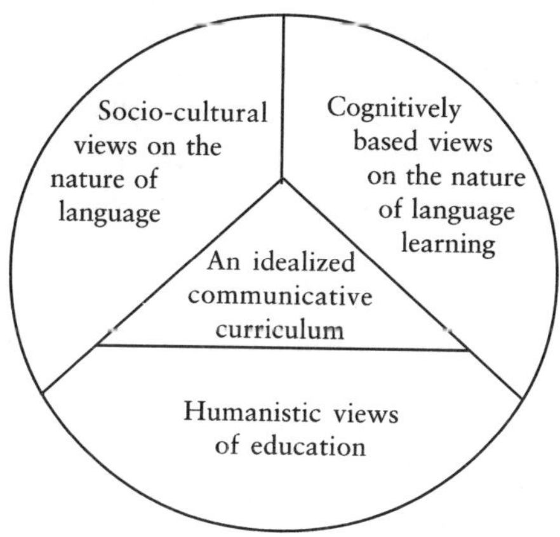

The major difference between a traditional curriculum (based on classical humanism) and a learner-centred curriculum (based on progressivism) is that the latter involves the learners and the teachers in the decision-making process of 'what,' 'why' and 'how' to teach. As Nunan says:

> This is particularly true of content selection and gradation. These will need to be modified during the course programme delivery as the learners' skills develop, their self-awareness as learners grows, and their perceived needs change.[10]

A learner-centred curriculum bases itself on the methodology and the principles of teaching/learning process "which are clearly designated to bring about a classroom where enquiry, activity, discussion, reflection and open-ended personal interpretations feature rather than predetermined objectives, content and mastery level."[11]

Hutchinson and Waters rightly point out that learning is not just a mental process but a process of negotiation between individuals and society.[12] Majority of the learners undertake language study for reasons which arise directly or indirectly out of perceived needs of the community to which they belong. Moreover, their language study will be "conducted within an educational framework which is shaped by the socio-economic conditions of their home community and which will also reflect the attitudes, beliefs and tradition of this community. Contextual factors of this nature play a significant role in creating the learning environment in which language study will occur. Consequently, learner-centred teaching has to be pursued in a socially and contextually sensitive manner in harmony with the traditions and expectations of the community within which teaching takes place."[13]

In India, a non-native variety of English flourishes which is termed the 'Indian English.' The effect of this non-native institutionalized variety on the teaching and learning of English cannot be ignored. It determines the model to be taught, selection of authentic materials and even the very notion of 'communicative competence.' Thus, one's communicative competence—whether it means the prepositional meaning, the elocutionary force or the interpretative capacity, i.e. procedures for negotiating meaning or all three together is to be determined with reference to this non-native form. For learners in these situations the 'authentic'[14] target language materials are not those written overseas but those which they find around them in the daily newspapers, journals, radio, television—to which they are exposed in their daily lives. This non-native variety naturally clashes with the standard variety to which they are exposed in the classrooms. It is then the non-native form which comes naturally to them both because of their daily experience and the pull of their mother tongue. Besides, this non-native form may have come to be associated with their identity and any attempt to initiate the native form may be regarded as pedantic. Kachru rightly argues that interactive acts are determined by the contexts of culture and context of situation. What appears lexically, collocutionally and semantically, deviant from native speakers' point of view, is culturally and situationally appropriate from non-native speaker's angle.[15]

Nativisation is, therefore, a natural linguistic process and cannot be stopped. Moreover, the needs of the society have also to be kept in view. As Banerji rightly remarks, "The main focus of such syllabus can be oriented to take care of the central purpose of language teaching, namely imparting communicative competence and thus fulfils the requirements of society and the demands of education."[16]

Contextual factors, therefore, cannot be ignored. These relate to the practical conditions under which teaching and learning will be conducted. These will include the class size, quantity of both teaching and learning facilities available, administrative and decision-making structures already existing in a given set-up together with the learning culture and traditions of learning present in the educational system and in the community as a whole. Kennedy stresses this point by saying that the patterns of behaviour at classroom level can only be fully understood in the light of the socio-cultural forces at work in the community at large. Kennedy illustrates this with the help of the following diagram:[17]

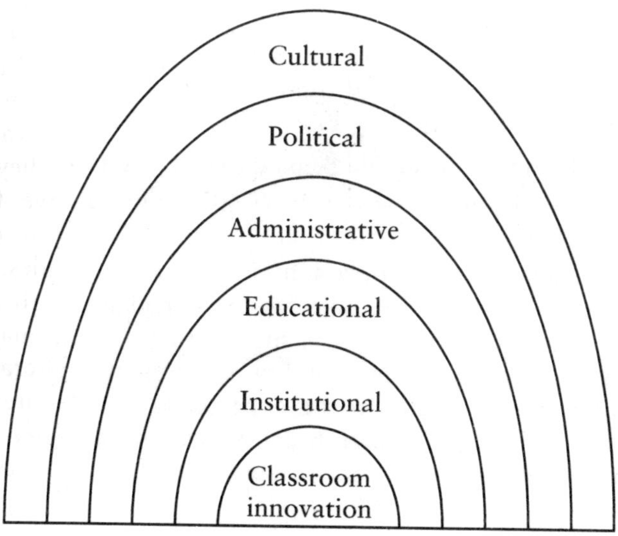

Tudor calls the cultural, political and administrative factors which shape the educational context as 'means analysis' whereas the attitudes with which learners come to the class and which is a product of their socio-cultural environment as 'classroom culture.'

Both these sets of factors play a vital role. They provide "...guidelines as to what is ecologically appropriate and sustainable in the local context."[18] Singh feels that "apart from information on factors like sociolinguistic settings, local circumstances, government policy and management at departmental and institutional level, a knowledge of their (students') educational background, aspirations and attitudes to language learning and teaching and their expectations of an English class is equally vital for a meaningful language planning."[19]

These factors need, therefore, to be borne in mind throughout the planning of any new course or approach to teaching, especially if this involves methodological procedures which are novel to the target institution or community. Rubin feels that "the learning tradition in which learners have grown up can exert a powerful influence on how they will expect learning to be structured and on what they consider to be useful learning activities."[20]

It is, therefore, important to evaluate the behavioural implications of a pedagogical innovation and how they relate to the expectations and value systems of the given community.

Particular attention should be paid to learners' (and society's) attitudes to authority, teacher-learner roles and the concept of self-direction.[21]

A learner-centred approach with its communicative methodology is highly desirable from the pedagogic point of view but it will also create problems. These problems will not only arise out of the incompatability of the methodology with the syllabus but also due to the expectations of the students and teachers which will have been shaped by the established educational set-up.

In moving from a traditional approach to a communicative approach we will be "...doing far more than substituting one set of materials for another—it will be attempting to replace one set of behaviours for another."[22] A learner-centred approach to teaching will alter a number of very practical aspects of course planning, a fact which needs to be borne in mind by both the teachers and the educational authorities.

Heavy demands will be imposed upon the teachers. They will need to be familiar with a wide range of teaching-learning options and should also understand the implications of these options. Not only will the syllabus be more learner-oriented and based on the needs of the learners but the materials used and the means of implementing them in the classroom will change together with the attitudes of both teachers and learners. Each will be discussed in detail.

Syllabus Design

All communicative methods use process-syllabuses which are less concerned with specifying content of output and more concerned with the sort of learning activities in which the learners have to engage themselves. They, therefore, align themselves more with methodology than with syllabus design. In such syllabuses, specification is more in terms of tasks and problems for the learner to grapple with them in terms of linguistic items. Proponents of the process approach are Breen and Candlin,[23] Prabhu,[24] Long,[25] Long and Crookes,[26] Allen,[27] Yalden,[28] Nunan[29] and Hutchinson and Waters.[30]

All process-syllabuses take the learner as their main focal point. The syllabus is based on the needs of the learners. The most thorough and widely known work on needs analysis is John Munby's *Communicative Syllabus Design*. Munby presents a highly detailed set of procedures for discovering target situation needs. He calls this set of procedures the Communication Needs Processor (CNP). The CNP consists of a range of questions about key communicative variables (topics, participants, medium, etc.) which can be used to identify the target language needs of any group of learners. Though the model gave a detailed account of 'what' to teach, it ignored the issue of 'how' to teach. It, therefore, based itself on data 'about' the learner rather than 'from' the learner and, therefore, it is argued that the model is only superficially learner-centred. Analysis of target needs involves far more than simply identifying the linguistic features of the target situation. It also involves taking into consideration what Hutchinson and Waters call 'lacks' and 'wants'[31] and what Richterich[32] calls 'objective' and 'subjective needs.' Brindley, taking up the distinction made by Richterich, elaborates further that the objective needs can be diagnosed by teachers on the basis of personal data obtained from learners whereas the subjective needs including wants, desires, expectations, etc., cannot be easily stated and diagnosed.

The 'objective' and the 'subjective' needs will put the learners at every stage in the design process. Course design will, therefore, become a negotiated process. No single factor will have a final influence on the content of the course. One of the purposes of subjective needs analysis is to involve learners and teachers in exchanging information so that the agenda of the teacher and the leaner may be more closely aligned. This will be done in two ways. In the first place, information provided by learners can be used to guide the selection of content and learning activities. Secondly, by providing learners with detailed information about goals, objectives and learning activities, learners will have a greater appreciation and acceptance of their learning experiences. The ESP learning situation and the target situation will both influence and be influenced by the nature of the syllabus, material, methodology and evaluation procedures. The course design will not move in a linear fashion. It will be a dynamic process wherein feedback channels will be incorporated into the whole design. The course design is represented in the diagram[33] that follows:

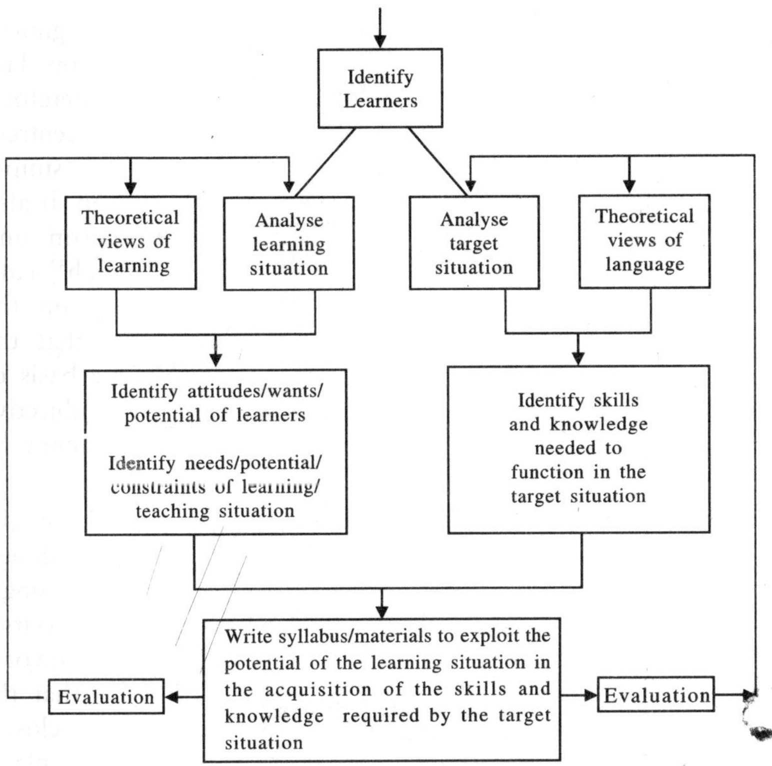

Instead of using the syllabus as the initial and once-and-for-all determiner of the content of materials and methodology, syllabus and materials evolve together with each being able to inform the other. In this way the syllabus is used creatively as a generation of interesting and relevant learning activities rather than as just a statement of language content which restricts and impoverishes the methodology. Yet at the same time it maintains relevance to target needs. It, therefore, serves the needs of the students both as users and learners of the language. Bell[34] also suggests a similar kind of course design:

> Communicative goals have produced profound changes in the three dimensions of a syllabus, namely the 'language content,' the 'process zone' and the 'product area.' This has been illustrated in the diagram[35] that follows.

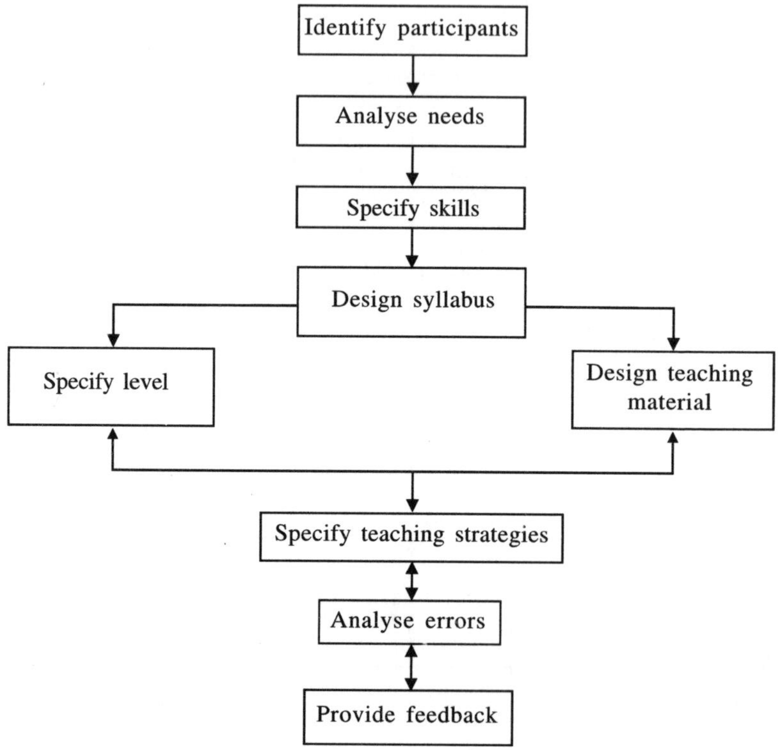

Although the communicative approach may not always create radical changes, it has affected our view of the way in which course outcomes are presented, defined and evaluated.[36]

Communicative syllabus design may be either functional-analytic which defines objectives in terms of categories of communicative language use or it may be non-analytical and experimental (natural growth hypothesis) which "takes the experiential here-and-now as the teaching focus rather than the external and fixed curriculum."[37]

Candlin advocates an interactive syllabus which is social and problem-solving in its orientation rather than knowledge based. It gives scope to participants "to ask questions from the outset about syllabus objectives, content, methodology and experiences and their evaluation. Moreover, the model is productive rather than merely reflective, in that it is through

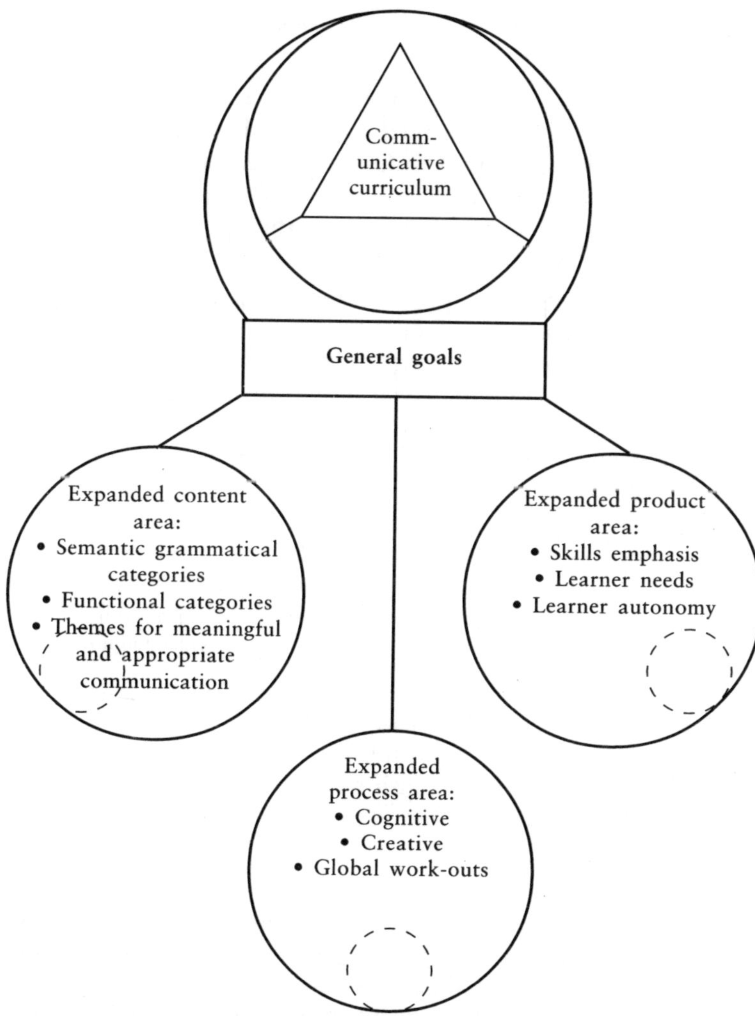

such questioning that new knowledge can be created and brought to bear in turn upon the entire syllabus process."[38]

Breen talks of a process syllabus which "would directly activate and encourage the creative construction and reinterpretation of subject matter by the participants in the classroom. Such a plan will provide a basis for the discovery of various routes for learning and thereby generate the actual classroom syllabus in a publically shared and explicit way."[39]

It offers a framework within which individual learners in the classroom can directly participate in the creation of plans.

Both Candlin and Breen are against a fixed and defined syllabus. Instead, they regard the syllabus as 'open' and 'negotiable.' They assist learners to draw their own route maps.[40] Breen and Candlin feel that "since learners are the main consumers of the materials, it is they who should decide the 'what' and 'how' of teaching."

Yalden proposes a 'proportional' syllabus. She favours developing a "type of programme consisting of a number of connected segments, each with a different focus which will operate in a cycle and which may be varied to suit the requirements of any situation."[41] The units can be 'recycled' or 'reoriented' for different learners in different situations. The shape of the syllabus will evolve from the way the teacher transposes it in her given situation. Yalden suggests the training of teachers to produce language courses with a highly communicative orientation. The job of the teacher will have to be "to accomplish the task of transposing (the framework provided) linguistically and culturally into the situation for which they are designing their course."[42]

Prabhu proposes a 'procedural' syllabus which is "...concerned with creating conditions for coping with meaning in the classroom to the exclusion of any deliberate regulation of the development of grammatical competence or a mere stimulation of language behaviour."[43] Brumfit who himself monitored the project in 1981 tells how it works:

> The programme is constructed around a series of problems, requiring the use of English, which have to be solved by the learners. The problems are introduced as specific tasks in which students have to interpret language data.... Tasks are usually preceded by pre-task, in which the teacher performs a task similar to the one that students will be asked to perform themselves, in interaction with the class, using whatever language seems appropriate for this purpose.... Following the pre-task and the task there is normally some direct evaluation in which learners discover whether they have successfully solved the problem but they receive no international evaluation of the English they have produced.[44]

Van EK gives a detailed account of the various syllabus components which need to be considered in developing language courses. He lists the following as necessary components of a language syllabus:

(1) The situation in which the foreign language will be used including the topics which will be dealt with.

(2) The language activities in which the learners will engage.[45]

Communicative goals are not restricted to conversation. All social uses of language including the reading of scientific and technical literature or of literary text whatever popular or classical are communicative:

> The priority afforded to communicative goals does not exclude the development of units devoted to the consolidation of the learners' understanding and mastery of the formal linguistic system (e.g., grammar, intonation, phonetics) but such units should not predominate in such a way as to evaluate intellectualized knowledge about the language above the ability to use it.[46]

In Widdowson's term "to describe communicative function in dissociation from the set of generative rules which realize it is to cut communication off from its cause and effect in system." In fact the two must be meaningfully related to escape from the situation in which "learners are being provided with language teaching programmes which attempt to develop communicative behaviour in dissociation from a knowledge of system and its meaning potential which can alone ensure that what is learned really, is a capacity for communication and not simply a collection of form/function correlates."[47]

Material Selection

The syllabus includes the conceptual functional components. It is no longer related to structural aspects alone. Clark feels that "...it would seem sensible to work towards a model in which it is possible to integrate them all and at the same time leave space for individual interpretations as to the exact balance to be struck between them according to the context."[48] No one, however, can produce a functional course without also teaching language forms. It is not a question of choosing to teach either structure or function. Both have to be taught. Cunningsworth[49] too, is of the view that it does not matter whether the material is wholly structural or wholly functional. What matters is how we teach the effective use of language in a context of social interaction.

Allen proposes an integrated model in which the content is derived from the other subjects on the curriculum. The aim is to integrate content language and language learning by basing all the materials on 'authentic,' topic-related information. The materials will "...provide practice in grammar, vocabulary and pronunciation as well as in functional and discourse features of language related to the subject area. At the same time they develop subject area skills by representing relevant content information, providing opportunities for concept development and providing practice in specialized techniques...."[50] The ESL modules provide training in English in association with other school subjects and thereby "infuse important themes and topics of educationally worthwhile content and substance into the otherwise conventional language class."[51] The 'vertical dimension' (linguistic component) of syllabus planning to use Allen's words is wedded with the 'horizontal dimension' (factual information) in an ESL module. The ESL module can be represented in the Allen-Howard model[52] that follows.

The language syllabus and the content syllabus both feed into classroom methodology which contains three interconnected activity components: (A) structural practice, which focuses on the formal features of the language (grammar, vocabulary etc.); (B) functional practice, which consists of controlled communicative activities; and (C) experiential practice, which is organised entirely in terms of task being undertaken or the message being conveyed. This is wholly fluency-oriented and not subject to any kind of linguistic control.

In the diagram, below the three methodology components or focal areas, are joined by paths which can be traversed in either direction to form a cycle of activities. In addition, we can go round any one of the circles any number of times or leave out one or two circles altogether. We can sometimes have

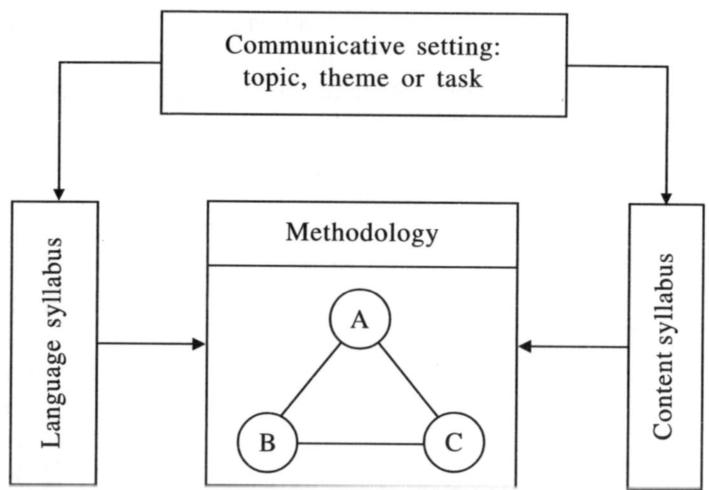

a single focus programme which would consist entirely of the structural or the functional on the experienced segment; a dual-focus programme which would consist of any two segments or a trifocal programme which would contain all the segments in equal balance or in asymmetrical cycles. The combination of three focal areas together with the principles of cyclicity and iteration allow for infinite variation in the organization of classroom activities. In every case the aim is to provide a rich learning environment with the widest possible range of materials for (systematic and non-systematic; knowledge-oriented and skill-oriented; authentic, simulated and controlled) a suitable balance, depending upon the proficiency level of the students. There is a built-in flexibility which enables us to provide maximum scope for individual teacher and student differences.

Hutchinson and Waters suggest a material model that is, "clear and systematic but flexible enough to allow for creativity and variety."[53] The model consists of four elements: 'input' 'content focus,' 'language focus,' 'task.' 'Input' provides the learners with the data based on their needs. The 'input' provides the material for classroom activities, new language items, correct models of language use, a topic for communication. The 'content' provides the non-linguistic content conveying information. 'Language-focus' focuses the attention of the learners on the language being used. 'Task' puts the learners to the actual use of the language in performing communicative acts.

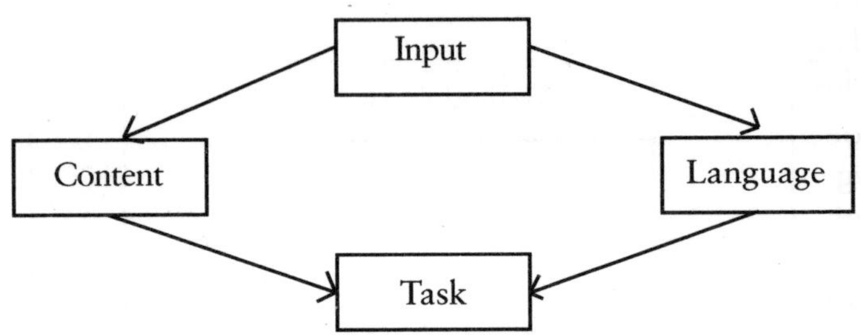

The primary focus of the unit is the task. The model acts as a vehicle which leads the learners to the point where they are able to carry out the task. The language and content are selected according to what the learners will need in order to do the task.

Brown and Yule suggest that materials can be made interesting by using them in an interesting way:

> It is, in principle not possible to find material which would interest everyone. It follows that the emphasis should be moved from attempting to provide intrinsically interesting materials which we have just claimed; it is generally impossible to doing interesting things with materials.... These materials should be chosen not so much on the basis of their own interest but for what they can be used to do.[54]

Hutchinson and Waters show how one text that was found in Penguin Book of the Natural World was converted into an interesting material for the language class. The original text reads as follows:

In the body's blood system, the heart is the pump that does the vital job of circulating the blood to all parts of the body. The tubes or blood vessels which carry blood from the heart are known as arteries; the blood vessels that return the blood to the heart are the veins. The heart is really two pumps side by side. Each pump sucks blood from veins into a collecting chamber the atrium or auricle, which then pushes the blood under high pressure into the ventricle below it. The ventricles pump the blood under high pressure into arteries. The pulse, which can be felt at various parts of the body, is caused by the simultaneous pumping action of the two ventricles.

Blood that has given up its oxygen to the tissues (deoxygenated blood) enters the heart through the right atrium. The right ventricle that pumps it to the lungs. Here it collects oxygen and returns through the veins to the left side of the heart to be pumped to the rest of the body before returning to the right atrium again. The double circulation is needed because the pressure at which the oxygenated blood leaves the lungs is too low. The pressure has to be boosted by re-pumping through the heart, so that it can press round the body just enough to supply the body tissues with the necessary oxygen.

A very important role is played by small flaps of skin of the heart and between the auricles and ventricles; these are one way valves that prevent the blood going the wrong way. If these valves are faulty it has a serious effect on the health of the person.[55]

Hutchinson and Waters[56] simplified it and made it interesting for the language class.

Input:

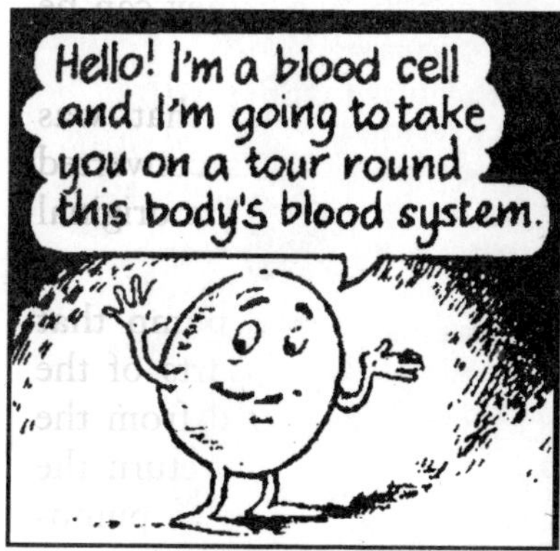

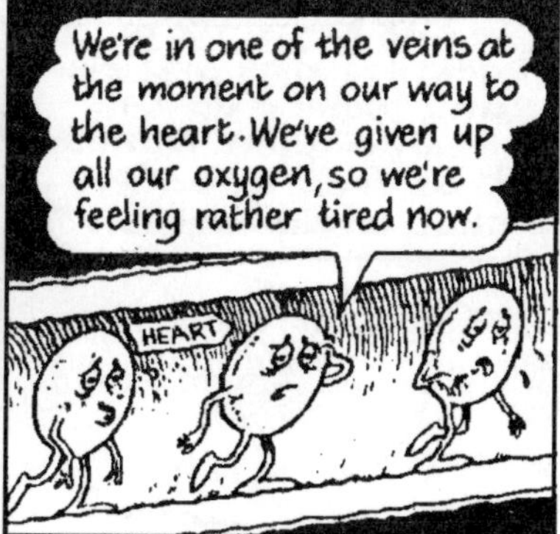

We're going into the heart through a valve and into the right auricle. This is like a collecting chamber and then we'll be sucked into the right ventricle.

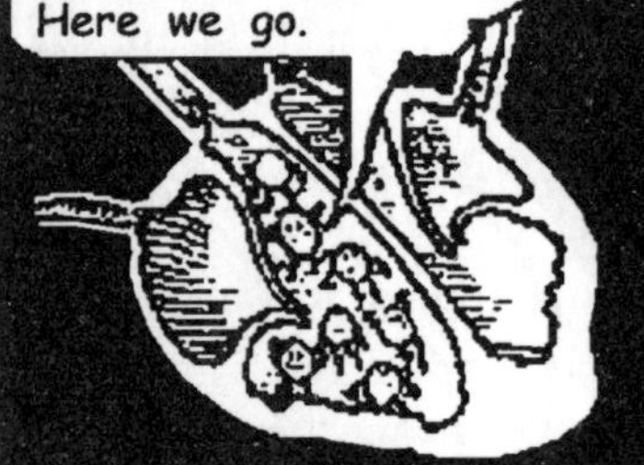
Here we are now in the ventricle. The heart muscles are starting to contract, so the pressure here is quite high now, We're about to be pumped into one of the arteries to take us to the lungs. Here we go.

We've just arrived in the lungs. We're getting nice and clean and picking up the fresh oxygen. Mmmm, that feels good. All that lovely oxygen.

We've got our oxygen now, but before we go off round the body we have to go back to the heart. You see, after going through the lungs we're not at a high enough pressure to take us all round the body. So the heart has to boost the pressure.
HEART
LUNGS
Here we are in the heart again, but this time in the left side, all ready to be pumped into the arteries. You will have guessed by now that the heart is really two pumps side by side.

This is where we leave the heart. We're just coming through the outlet from the left ventricle. We're at a very high pressure now. But we've got a long way to go, giving our oxygen to the tissue. Bye!

Language used was context and content-based. Language and content were both used to perform different communicative tasks in the classroom. While selecting the material to be taught in the classroom we have to consider how far the materials will harmonize with our learners' current and changing perceptions of their language learning needs.

Rivers and Melvin[57] have pointed out that if learning is to come about, then learning tasks need to be attuned to the cognitive style of the learners. Meeting needs arising from individual differences in cognitive style would, therefore, involve on the one hand exploiting the strategies learners already have (like rote learning and memorization) and on the other assisting them to acquire new strategies.

Little John remarks that:

> If we wish to involve learners more in the running of a language course then we need to devise tasks and materials that specifically develop the learners' ability to choose. Such tasks could involve learners in thinking more deeply about what they need to study and how they need to study.[58]

Any materials ought to provide a bridge between what our learners currently know and can do and the ultimate aims of the cause. Materials have to be evaluated and selected thoroughly before implementing them. They are not as Hutchinson says, "Simply the every day tools of the language teacher, they are an embodiment of the aims, values and methods of the particular teaching/learning situation."[59]

Material selection has to be a two-way process which enables teachers not just to select a textbook but also to develop their awareness of their own teaching/learning situation. It is necessary for the materials evaluator to look not only at the materials to be evaluated but also to carry out a thorough analysis of the teaching/learning situation that the materials are required for. A second concern for evaluating the relevance of materials in the appropriateness of their content to the personal interests of learners. The materials should develop the affective involvement of the learners in their learning so that learning is facilitated.

We need also to evaluate how well the materials meet the challenge of differentiation in learners' needs for using and developing skills and abilities.

Cunningsworth feels that:

> If we are to get away from the claustrophobic situation of using language for its own sake, we need to see that the materials which we adopt make use of language in order to convey information, express opinions, etc. which are of genuine intrinsic interest to the learners.[60]

As most learners find it difficult to articulate their needs and preferences, the initial stages of a course can be spent in providing a range of learning experiences. This can be done by developing a critical self-awareness using the mother tongue.

Brink *et al.* report that a group of teachers (who had considerable experience in learner-centred curriculum development) found that:

> At the 1+ (intermediate) level most learners can state their needs reasonably clearly if given the right opportunity. I'm convinced that if learners feel that you have listened sympathetically to their perceived needs and discussed your views of the situation with them then they have a far more committed and active role in the learning process—they are, in fact in control of their own learning, particularly if the consultation process is ongoing.[61]

Brindley feels that there should be negotiation and consultation between the teacher and the students but "this is not to suggest that the teacher should give learners everything that they want—evidence from teachers suggests that some sort of compromise is usually possible but only after there has been discussion concerning what both parties believe and want."[62]

If learners are not educated about the objectives of the language class, there may appear a conflict between the intentions of the teacher and those of the learners. As Allwright says, "...that instruction may well, much of the time, not make sense from the learner's perspective because it is fundamentally incomprehensible!"[63]

For this reason learners need to be trained as to how to get involved in their language study. This learner training can be given at the beginning of a course what Tudor calls 'training block' or alongside the course what he calls the 'ongoing slot':

> Over time, as learner's understanding of language learning increases, learner training will give way to learner involvement, i.e. "the negotiation and joint selection of learning content and form which is the essence of a learner-centred approach to course development."[64]

Apart from implementing a change in learners' attitudes and making them aware of their new roles, we have to look to their language needs and educational goals as well. But as Van EK believes:

> It is neither feasible nor desirable for the expert group to attempt to frame once and for all a canonical set of language learning objectives. It isn't possible to foresee the needs of all audience or the characteristic learning situations. Such a scheme would inevitably be subject-based rather than learner-centred and be in grave danger of imposing oppressive strains on the development of rationalized language learning, what is required is a flexible supportive structure which will enable discussions on the objectives and methods of language learning to be decentralized—made on each occasion by the parties involved in the light of understanding of the particular circumstances, especially the need characteristics of the learners-concerned.[65]

Our learners being General English Learners, we shall primarily wish to provide them with the ability to communicate in general circumstances about general subjects of general importance and interest. Ingram talks of 'General English Ability' which can be defined as the ability to carry out commonly occurring real world tasks.

However varied concrete manifestations may be, Van EK feels that, "...communication and language each have a hard common core, a core that forms the backbone of language use whatever the topic may be. With respect to communication this core is constituted by the general communicative functions such as stating, asking, denying, correcting, expressing doubt, expressing ability, willingness, etc., together with such general notions as presence/absence, before and after past/present/future, causality, contrast, etc....whatever topic of communication we choose and practise, the learners will inevitably be exposed to the common core both of communication and of language. In other words, in the prespective of the acquisition of general communicative ability *the actual choice of topics is of secondary importance* as long as this common core which is the basis of transfer potential is adequately present"[66] (emphasis mine). What is, therefore, important is not so much the topics that are chosen as the way in which they are implemented in the language class. The same view is expressed by Prabhu who feels it more important to create conditions for communicating rather than develop grammatical competence.

Long and Crookes[67] find 'two way tasks' in which two participants must share information in order to complete a task or solve a problem, effective in stimulating the development of communication skills. In particular, such activities provide an environment for the development of fluency and the negotiation of meaning. They also stimulate learners to mobilise all their linguistic resources and push their linguistic knowledge to the limit. Long and Porter[68] suggest that small group work in the language classroom provides the optimum environment for negotiated comprehensible output. In providing a psycholinguistic rationale for group work Long and Porter cite both Krashen's 'comprehensible input'[69] and Swains' 'comprehensible output'[70] hypothesis. Group work provides an environment in which learners can comprehend. It gives them opportunities for production and it provides contexts within which meaning can be negotiated. It, therefore, involves student participation. Varonis and Gass[71] have demonstrated that there are advantages in arranging pair work between learners of different proficiency levels. Harmer favours pair work and group work because it has enormous potential for oral work, as also for reading and writing tasks.

Di Pietro stresses the use of dialogues and the teaching of idiomatic competence to second language learners. He finds it (idiomatic competence) very essential since without it even an advanced student would find himself "left right out in the cold in the target society."[72] Regarding dialogues, Di Pietro feels that the ability to engage successfully in a dialogue helps to develop communicative competence since a number of criteria are bought into play of which role-play is only one aspect. Each point of interchange in a dialogue is potentially a branching point giving the interlocutors enough choice between a number of alternative continuations or strategies. The 'dialogue with options' can be built around any situation in which different options could be adopted. The teacher can provide the class with a stem and provide the learners with cue cards. Besides, as Revell points out that "three or four line dialogues which express feelings as well as facts provide excellent intonation practice."[73]

Besides using 'dialogues with options', the teacher can use role-play activities. Role-play means 'learning by doing' and experiments reveal that it is an extremely effective way of learning.[74] It calls for a total response from the player: "It asks him to communicate—to respond verbally - and non-verbally and it exploits his knowledge and experience outside the classroom, his common stock of knowledge."[75] Moreover, role-play can be very motivating since there is a game instinct involved. Also it provides the learners with a specification of 'what' kind of things to say in 'what' message forms 'to what' kinds of people 'in what' situations (Hymes definition of communicative competence).

Rath believes that "one activity is more worthwhile than another.... If it assigns to students active roles in the learning situations rather than passive ones...if it involves children with realia...if it is relevant to the expressed purposes of the students."[76]

All these activities are only possible in an atmosphere which is relaxed and without any inhibitions and anxieties. Revell feels that classroom activities like "...games, group and pair exercises are intended to loosen up the class and create a relaxed and harmonious atmosphere conducive to role-play activities.... They relax a person physically and so make him less inhibited generally."[77]

Classroom arrangement (i.e., the arrangements of desks and chairs in the class) plays a vital role in creating the relaxed atmosphere that Revell talks of. In classroom with fixed desks all facing forwards in rows, group work is difficult. Moreover, Revell says, "If teaching is to be truely communicative then it goes without saying that the teacher should not be the focus of attention all the time."[78] Circular seating arrangement has a number of advantages—it brings every student in contact with the rest of the class and the teacher and provides a large space in the centre to perform various activities that might need a lot of space.

New Learner's Roles

Since Communicative Method is learner-centred, it gives a pivotal role to the learner in all decision-making processes from the initial needs analysis to the framing of the syllabus. New demands are put on the learner and his/her roles change. "The implication for the learner is that he should contribute as much as he gains and thereby learn in an interdependent way."[79]

Maley also finds the learners in a new role where "they (the learners) will no longer find it enough to follow the lesson passively but will need to involve themselves as real people in the activities they are asked to undertake both inside and outside the classroom."[80]

Active learner's involvement can be demanding and if learner's motivation and commitment to language study is limited or constrained by other factors, they may be unable or unwilling to fit into a learner-centred approach which they may find as confusing and disconcerting.

Our students come to the class with fixed preconceived ideas. They look upon the teacher as a kind of *guru* from whom all knowledge flows. They are accustomed to the lecture mode of teaching with the teacher lecturing in front of a class of about 100-150 students which form one large lockstep group. Though the least demanding of the students and the teachers, it has various grave disadvantages. One of the chief disadvantages is that, however impressive the teacher might appear, it is impossible to sustain the interest of the pupils for a long time. Moreover, the teacher always guesses about the effectiveness of his lecture because there is very little chance of receiving feedback from the listeners. This can be overcome to some extent by allowing the students to express their views on the lecture or by asking comprehensive questions or even by giving a one-minute written quiz everyday at the end of the class. However, with all the efforts that we make, we will only be able to make the bright students talk. The shy and dull students will not speak.

A shift is, therefore, required from a referential to an inferential mode of learning. This can lead to some degree of disorientation. The fluency and task-based activities like 'playing games' or 'acting out non-classroom roles,' 'having fun' or 'managing without the teacher' may embarrass them at first and conflict with the norms of formal education and with what Prabhu called the 'classroom ethos.'[81] Such problems arise with learners (and teachers) whose expectations and attitudes have been shaped by the established educational orthodoxy which informs conventional pedagogy, not only in English teaching but in the other subjects in the curriculum. One cannot expect that learners will very readily adopt a pattern of behaviour in the English class which is at variance with the roles they are required to play in their other lessons. This should not be taken as a serious threat. The students can gradually be conditioned to these activities by gradually releasing the control and making the learners fully participate in the end.

Paulston[82] and Rivers[83] see the learner moving from controlled practice through guided work to free communication with an increasing emphasis on choice of what to say along the way.

Littlewood[84] too has argued for a mixture of pre-communicative and communicative activities moving from the controlled to the free, with a focus on form function and social meaning which teachers would draw upon in order to respond to the learners' need of the moment.

Brumfit[85] makes a similar proposal suggesting that 'accuracy' work should occupy a large proportion of an initial language course but should gradually decrease in importance in favour of 'fluency' work. Both, however should be judiciously mixed in response to learner needs. Oxford and Ehrman suggest that learners need to be extended beyond their stylistic comfort zone even if it is important to do so in a *gradual and sensitive manner*[86] (emphasis mine).

Not only do the learners need to be conditioned in using communicative techniques in the class, they also need to be made aware of how to evaluate their own progress and to determine for themselves the extent to which the results achieved are in line with their objectives: "It is this crucial evaluation centred on the learning for which the learner must assume responsibility that amounts to real self-evaluation."[87]

Upshur feels that the best way to measure someone's oral proficiency is simply to ask him how well he speaks the language.

This self-evaluation of learning[88] like that of acquisition will be carried out on the basis of personal criteria such as the compatibility between the proposed methods and techniques and the external constraints (availabilities of place and time; physical possibilities, etc.) and internal constraints (intellectual and physical ability, etc.). As Henner Stanchina and Holec state:

> As a language learner one needs feedback and input information on learning strategies, learning techniques, etc., in other words, on the suitability and effectiveness of learning in relation to personal learning criteria and personal goals. This information will increase the learner's awareness of how he learns and helps him make decisions as to the continuation or modification of his learner activities.[89]

The individual student has to be brought to an efficient realization of his own achievement or lack of it in relation to the goals he sets for himself. This implies that he should have available to him not only the means of assessing his own performance but also the means of learning how to make the assessments. This shift in emphasis has resulted in a redirection of interest from norm-referenced tests, i.e. tests where the learner's performance is matched against that of other learners to criterion-referenced tests where the learner's performance is matched against some predetermined criteria. Rivers is of the view that the latter type of tests has the advantage that matching against the criterion becomes a challenge and a guide to further effort instead of a hurdle to be surmounted.[90]

Rivers goes on to say that in using criterion-referenced tests "the student knows exactly what knowledge he must demonstrate and either demonstrates it and moves on or cannot demonstrate it and goes back to see how he can improve his performance."[91]

Criterion-referenced tests and performance objective thus facilitate the adaptation of instruction to individual goals and the learner can assume more responsibility for his own training so that "when he feels ready to match the criteria he tests. Note that *he* tests; it is not we who test him. If necessary he later re-tests. When satisfied that he has matched the criterion he moves on."[92]

This philosophy, Trim feels, matches with the overall philosophy of "a learner-centred needs and motivation-based language learning system"[93] as well as with the notion of self-assessment.

Tests have to be integrated into the learning process, chiefly in order to provide feedback to the learners and they ought to be controlled where feasible by the learners. They serve a variety of functions, e.g. 'placement tests' help to allocate the learners to an appropriate group; 'progress tests' give information to the learner and teacher as to whether learning is taking place as planned so that the programme can be modified; 'achievement tests' ascertain whether the learner has achieved the terminal course objectives. This information helps to plan their next step. Rivers recommends criteria referenced tests where the individual is tested against a criteria and not tested in comparison with his classmates. Testing[94] is only one aspect of evaluation which involves more than just testing student outcomes. Evaluation on the other hand involves examining the various aspects of the teaching-learning process to get a better understanding of what is not effective, what is more effective and what appears to be of no use at all. Evaluation must therefore focus on both the means (process) and the product of the teaching-learning process.[95]

Evaluation is not therefore, a one-way process in which the teacher or an outsider assesses the performance of the learner on the basis of externally defined criteria. It is on the other hand, a dynamic process in which learners are involved interactively with others in the class firstly, in deciding on what to evaluate and secondly, in actually evaluating it. The feedback that both teacher and students receive in such a multi-way system would be meaningful and useful to the participants. Evaluation cannot, therefore be carried out in a static way with pre-determined external criteria but in negotiation with the different participants. This entails orienting and training the students to be able to evaluate in a systematic and principled way.

In fact, involving the learner in the evaluation process itself is a way of enabling him/her to do it well by actively participating in the teaching-learning-evaluation process. Learners will gradually internalise the nuances of the evaluation system and will be able to interpret the feedback in a way that is meaningful to them which would enable them to become better learners. As a result they will be better able to participate in the evaluation process instead of having it imposed on them by outsiders.

This self-assessment entails peer evaluation which is what is implied in interactive learning, a notion that communicative approaches strongly advocate. Peer evaluation enables evaluation to take place in a non-threatening way. We have often encountered the situation where evaluation has achieved frustration among the learners. It is largely because the evalution system treats learners as objects rather than as interactive, responsive participants in the learning process.

Teaching and evaluation are inextricably linked with each other and one feeds into the other. One significant feature of evaluation should be feedback. Feedback should be made integral to evaluation so that the learning-teaching process becomes more productive and meaningful.

Leblanc and Painchand point out that self-assessment needs to be linked in a direct and transparent manner to student's experience of the target language (TL). They feel that the assumption of responsibility for one's learning which is implicit in self-assessment can create problems with some students who feel that any type of evaluation should be the responsibility of someone in authority of someone who knows.[96] Tudor is also of the same opinion that...some learners can react negatively to the role and responsibilities implicit in self-assessment if these run counter to their attitudes to the learning process...self-assessment then, like other aspects of learners' involvement is an activity which learners *need guidance and time to grow into* (emphasis mine).[97]

Dr. Oskarsson sees training in self-assessment as having a positive influence on the general quality of learners' involvement in their language study and as a means of fostering their ability to assume an active and self-directive role in their learning.

Learner's Role

The acceptance of responsibility for the learning by the learner involves two fundamental changes in the context of learning—a change in the definition of knowledge to be acquired and a change in the learner/knowledge relationship. Van EK and Trim express this change as follows:

> ...this new learning context changes the learner/learning relationship. The position of passivity and dependence in which the learner was necessarily confined because the knowledge was not accessible to him without the help of an expert-teacher is no longer tenable.... It is no longer essential for the learning to be taken charge of by the teacher, the learner himself can assume responsibility for it.[98]

This acceptance of a new responsibility defining the learner's new role can only be possible if "the learner is willing and (if) ...he is also *capable* of assuming responsibility"[99] (emphasis mine).

Ian Tudor feels that our learners have been used to a content-based and teacher-led form of learning. They simply may not have had the opportunity to develop the skills that they need in order to assume a self-directive role in their own learning.[100]

Talking about the same problem Holec points out:

> ...few adults are capable of assuming responsibility for their learning...for the simple reason that they have never had occasion to use this ability. The knowledge and personal qualities that learner's involvement requires cannot be taken for granted. A learner-centred approach needs, therefore, to contain an element of awareness development in our learners.[101]

Learners' have to be trained for their new roles. Learner's training needs to be integrated with language study activities. The goal is to develop what Wenden describes as a critical and informed awareness[102] of learning options. Dubin and Olshtain suggest that:

> Intermediate steps need to be provided that will act to imbue participants in a communicatively oriented course with an understanding of its underlying values. In effect, attitudes and expectations must change.... It means that part of the course design will be overtly directed to establishing new role identities that are more closely related to the purpose of communicative language use and which might be significantly different from the roles to which learners had been hitherto accustomed to.[103]

Holec suggests two processes needed to help learners to assume this self-directive role a gradual 'deconditioning process' which will cause the learner to break away...from the notion that there is one ideal method and teachers posesses that method and a gradual process of acquiring the knowledge and know-how he needs in order to assume responsibility for his learning, to learn to use tools such as dictionaries and grammar books...to learn to analyse his performance and so on.[104]

It is through the parallel operation of these two that we can proceed from a position of dependence to one of independence, from a non autonomous to an autonomous state which Trim feels "should be one of the built-in educational objectives of a learning programme."[105]

Brindley also feels, "many learners do have rather fixed ideas about what it is to be a learner and what it is to learn a language."[106] They are antipathetic towards classroom techniques and activities which can be described as 'communicative.' In consequence, communication language teachers who also subscribe to a learner-centred philosophy find themselves confronted with a dilemma when dealing with learners who have traditional attitudes and beliefs about what are appropriate classroom activities. Nunan suggests "that the way out of this dilemma must be in extensive consultation, negotiation and information exchange between the teacher and the learner."[107]

Teacher's Role

With a change in the learner's role, the teacher's role will automatically change. As Maley says:

> They can no longer be regarded as possessing sacrosant knowledge which they dispense in daily doses to their docile flock. Instead, they will need to set up tasks and activities in which the learners play the major overt role. It is then their job to monitor these activities and to modify and adjust them as time goes by.[108]

A teacher who is strongly committed to fostering self-direction in her students may find her students resistant to assuming an independent role and may want the teacher to play a more authoritative or directive role. Moreover, the teacher herself may be led to define her role "...in terms of the transmission of a pre-established body of knowledge enshrined in form of a grammatical or functional syllabus, a given examination or series of course books. For either or both of these reasons teachers may not have had the opportunity to develop the skills they need to manage a participative approach to course development comfortably."[109] This leads to what Wagner[110] calls 'knots.' These emerge when the teacher's training and her/his previous experience clash with the demands of the learner-centred mode of teaching.

Teachers who have been trained within a traditional approach to teaching and whose experience has been within a framework defined by adherence to a pre-established curriculum may find the new demands which the new approach places on them as unsettling "because there is a conflict or mismatch between old and new perceptions and, more seriously a threat to prevailing routines and to the sense of security dependent upon them."[111]

The teacher will find his job more varied and more challenging. As Van EK and Trim relate that:

> ...much greater demands will be made on his creativity than on his highly developed knowledge of teaching techniques. The traditional teacher who might have been regarded as 'replaceable' will give way to a teacher whose role in the process of developing the learner will no longer be based on the power conferred by hierarchial authority but on the quality and importance of his relationship to the learner.[112]

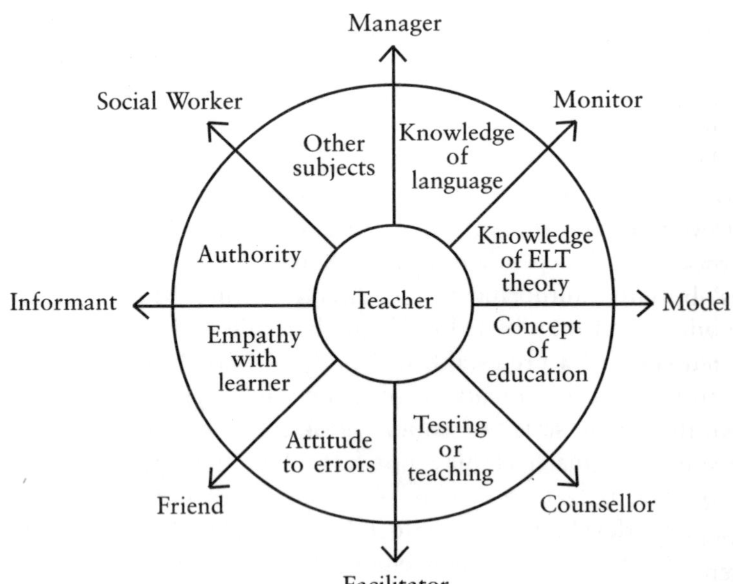

This new role is illustrated by Prodoromon in the diagram[113] which follows. The teacher is shown to be surrounded by a number of constraints (the inner circle) and once he overcomes these constraints he is shown to play various roles.

Harmer also assigns the teacher similar roles like "roles of the controller, assessor, prompter, participant and resourcer."[114]

This new role definition will give rise to an acute problem of teacher training as also other problems of an institutional nature which will be as practical and urgent. Gaies and Bowers mention a number of problems that will be faced by teachers due to:

— the adoption of new textbook;
— the introduction of methodological or pedagogical reforms that teachers have not been trained to implement;
— the establishment of new goals for a language teaching programme and the prescription of new teacher-learner role relationships in the classroom.[115]

In addition to these problems our teachers in the Kashmir valley as in the rest of India also face the problem of heterogeneity in the proficiency level of our students. The question arises whether we can frame a communicative syllabus based on the needs of the learners when the needs of the learners are as varied as their proficiency levels, i.e. not only do the learners greatly differ in their proficiency levels but they are also varied as regards to their needs which in most cases are not even clear to them. In other words, can the communicative method be applied in our appalling situations?[116] The answer is 'yes' but it cannot be done overnight. It will take time since the whole system has to be reframed. All the same it has to be started somewhere. The mere postponement of the method till we find congenial situations for its implementation will not solve the problem. It has to make a beginning somewhere and the sooner, the better.

Related to the problem of heterogeneity is the problem of unmanageable classroll. Various questions come to our mind when we think of applying the communicative method in our situation. Can the techniques advocated by the communicative method be applied in our class with the roll sometimes even extending to 150 students? Willey talking about the same issue feels, "whereas the language games may be received with enthusiasm by a class of twenty, it may be an utter failure in a class of fifty."[117] All the same he feels, "teachers who do not use games are neglecting one of the most vital of teaching practices."[118] We need therefore, to consider whether we can use group work, pair work, etc. in our situation. Can we reduce the classroll so that communicative techniques would be applicable? If the communicative method is applied outright will it not result in class indiscipline and management problems? Without the teacher's control, would it be desirable to leave a class of 150 students to interact on their own? Would not the 150 students talking freely make the classroom situation unmanageable? Is it therefore, advisable or desirable to apply the method in our situation? The answer to all these questions lies in the fact that we need not blame the method for the huge classroll. Instead, we need to reduce the classroll and make the method implemental. Instead of discarding the communicative method on account of huge classroll, we need to adjust our classroll and accommodate the method.

For any change to be successful, it has to be accepted by the teachers who will realise it. Acceptance involves "...being able to live comfortably with the practical consequences in terms of the professional demands it places on them and its consequences in terms of their social and interpersonal relationships with their students...."[119] From this perspective Tudor suggests "...the importance of catering for ongoing teacher development and support as an integral part of the implementation of a learner-centred approach to teaching."[120]

Wenden is also of the same view, "teacher education is an essential ingredient in the management of educational change. In the promotion of new methods and materials the teacher is the main change agent—not the materials or techniques in which innovations are packaged. Their acceptance and success will depend on the teacher...."[121]

In India, as in the Kashmir region, the teachers of English

are inadequately trained to teach English. A careful look at the B.Ed. (Secondary) teacher training syllabus followed by the Regional College of Education (National Council of Educational Research and Training) or the Department of Education, Delhi University, for that matter, reveals that it is heavily devoted to the theory of education and a very small part of the teacher-training course is given to the teaching of English. Teachers of English, unlike teachers in other subjects or even L1, need specialized training, for English is a second language in India. "The existing teacher training institutes in India," as Dr. Sood believes, "do not have well-equipped departments of English to cater to this need. In the existing set-up these play a secondary role and the curriculum is dominated by the department of education who feed the learners the theory of education—principles of education, educational psychology, history and development of education and so on."[122]

Unless this trend is reversed and a situation is created in which English teaching (for those learners specializing in the teaching of English) is given the status of the main subject with other subjects as secondary support subjects, the quality of trained English teachers is not likely to improve. "We could," as Dr. Sood suggests, "delink the training of teachers of English from the existing institutes of education and open institutes of English on the pattern of the CIEFL for imparting specialized training to existing and prospective teachers of English."[123] The CDC report (1989) emphasizes the teacher-training programmes in terms of developing the linguistic and communicative skills in teachers:

> Training courses for...teachers must...include components such as the structure of the English language and English language teaching and testing.[124]

To implement the Communicative Method, two kinds of changes will be involved. As Maley puts it:

> The first is institutional change. Unless syllabi, examinations, inspectors, textbooks, etc. reflect the declared desire to change in the direction of a more communicatively oriented

curriculum, little can result.... The second is teacher education. Change needs also to come from below, from the teachers who will have to implement it. This can only happen in two ways either through teacher training or through the efforts of the voluntary group of teachers who gather informally to offer help.[125]

That change from the present traditional method to the Communicative Method is possible, has already been reported by Pushpinder Syal[126] to have taken place in the Panjab University. The new syllabus aims at teaching oral communication skills, for instance, 'making enquiries,' 'supplying information', etc. in the classroom by involving students in real communication. A similar change has taken place in the Delhi University where the syllabus has been framed along communicative lines and has been found "appropriate in terms of texts chosen and tasks assigned."[127]

This implies that the communicative method is practical and implementable. But before generalizing, we should take our local situation into account and know the psychological readiness on the part of our students as well as teachers to accept this new method. We have to see whether or not they are ready to accept this novel method. It is to this issue that we shall turn now in the chapter that follows.

REFERENCES

1. Bjoin B., Jernudd and J.D. Gupta. "Towards a Theory of Language Planning" in Rubin & Jernudd (eds.). *Can Language Be Planned? Sociolinguistic Theory and Practice for Developing Nations.* Honolulus: The University Press of Hawon, 218.
2. Mackey in L.A. Jakobovits. *Foreign Language Learning: A Psycholinguistic Analysis of Issues.* Rowley, Mass: Newbury House, 1970, xii.
3. C.N. Candlin. "Syllabus Design as a Critical Process" in C.J. Brumfit (ed). *General English Syllabus Design. ELT Documents 118.* Council of Europe, 1984, 30.
4. H.G. Widdowson. "Educational Pedagogic Factors in Syllabus Design" in C.J. Brumfit (ed.). *ELT Documents 118.* 26.
5. H.G. Widdowson. "Design Principles for a Communicative Grammar" in C.J. Brumfit (ed.). *The Practice of Communicative Teaching. ELT Document* 124. 1986, 41.

6. J.P.B. Allen. "General-Purpose Language Teaching: A Variable Focus Approach" in C.J. Brumfit (ed.). *General English Syllabus Design. ELT Documents 118*. Council of Europe. 1984, 63.

7. J.P.B. Allen. "General-Purpose Language Teaching: A Variable Focus Approach" in *ELT Documents 118*. 61.

8. John L. Clark. *Curriculum Renewal in School Foreign Language Learning*. Oxford: Oxford University Press, 1987.

9. Dubin & Olshtain. *Course Design*. 68.

10. D. Nunan. *The Learner-Centred Curriculum*. Cambridge: Cambridge University Press, 1988, 5.

11. John L. Clark. *Curriculum Renewal in School Foreign Language Learning*. Oxford: Oxford University Press, 1987, 52.

12. T. Hutchinson's and A. Waters. *English for Specific Purposes*. Cambridge: Cambridge University Press, 1987, 82.

13. Ian Tudor. *Learner-Centredness as Language Education*. Cambridge: Cambridge University Press, 1996, 128-129.

14. 'Authentic' meaning 'life-like' and 'real.'

15. Braj B. Kachru (ed.). *The Other Tongue: English Across Cultures*. Oxford: Pergamon Press. 332.

16. Meera Banerji & Krishna Mohan. "General English Syllabuses: A Critical Review." *Journal of Higher Education* 10, 3, 243.

17. C. Kennedy. "Evaluation of the management of change in ELT projects." *Applied Linguistics* 9. 1988, 322.

18. *Ibid.*, 132.

19. R.K. Singh. "A Case of Syllabus Constraints in ELT." *The Journal of English Language Teaching* 17, 6: 187-92.

20. J. Rubin. 'What the Good Language Learner Can Teach Us.' *TESOL Quarterly* 9. 1975, 41-51.

21. Ian Tudor. *Learner-Centredness as Language Education*. 254.

22. C. Kennedy. "Innovating For a Change: Teacher Development and Innovation." *ELT Journal* 41. 1987, 166-7.

23. M.P. Breen and C.N. Candlin. "The Essentials of a Communicative Curriculum in Language Teaching." *Applied Linguistics* 1. 1980, 89-112.

24. N.S. Prabhu. "Procedural Syllabuses." Paper read at the *RELC Seminar* at Singapore. 1983.

25. M.H. Long. "A Role for Instruction in Second Language Acquisition" in Hyltenstam & Pienemann (eds.). *Modelling and Assessing Second Language Acquisition*. Clevedon: Multilingual Matters, 1985.

26. M.H. Long and G. Crookes. "Intervention Points in Second Language Classroom Processes." Paper presented at *RELC Seminar* at Singapore. 21-26, April 1986.

27. J.P.B. Allen. "A Three-Level Curriculum Model For Second Language Education." *Canadian Modern Language Review* 40(1). 23-43.
28. J. Yalden. *The Communicative Syllabus: Evolution Design and Implementation.* Oxford: Pergamon Press, 1983.
29. D. Nunan. *The Learner-Centred Curriculum: A Study in Second Language Teaching*. Cambridge: Cambridge University Press, 1988.
30. T. Hutchinson and A. Waters. *English for Specific Purposes.* Cambridge: Cambridge University Press, 1987.
31. Hutchinson and Waters, 1987, 58.
32. R. Richterich (ed.). *Case Studies in Identifying Language Needs.* Oxford: Pergamon Press, 1983.
33. Hutchinson & Waters, 1987, 74.
34. Roger T. Bell. *An Introduction to Applied Linguistics.* London: Batsford, 1981, 950.
35. Dubin & Olshtain. *Course Design*, 89.
36. This will be discussed in detail in Chapter 4.
37. Leon A. Jackobovits and Barbara Gordon. *The Context of Foreign Language Teaching*. Rowley, Mass: Newbury House, 1974, 44.
38. C.N. Candlin. "Syllabus Design as a Critical Process." *ELT Documents* 118, 34.
39. M.P. Breen. "Process Syllabuses For The Language Classroom." *ELT Documents* 118, 58.
40. Quoted in H.H. Stern. "Review and Discussion." *ELT Documents* 118, 8.
41. Quoted in J.P.B. Allen. "General -Purpose Language Teaching: A Variable Focus Approach" in *ELT Documents* 118, 68.
42. J. Yalden. "An Interactive Approach to Syllabus Design. The Frameworks Project" in *ELT Documents* 124, 33.
43. N.S. Prabhu. *Second Language Pedagogy.* Oxford: Oxford University Press, 1987, 1-2.
44. C. Brumfit. *Communicative Methodology in Language Teaching: The Roles of Fluency and Accuracy.* Cambridge: Cambridge University Press. 1984, 104.
45. J. Van EK. *The Threshold Level in a European Unit/Credit System for Modern Language Learning by Adults.* Council for Cultural Co-operation. Council of Europe, 1975, 8-9.
46. J. Van EK & J.L.M. Trim. *Across the Threshold.* Pergamon Press: Council of Europe, 1984, 20.
47. H.G. Widdowson. "The Acquisition and Use of Language Systems." Paper delivered at the Berne Colloquium in *Applied Linguistics*, 1978, 10.
48. John. L. Clark. *Curriculum Renewal in School Foreign Language learning.* 53.

49. Alan Cunningsworth. *Evaluating and Selecting EFL Teaching Materials.* London: Heinemann Educational Books, 1984, 16.
50. J.P.B. Allen. "Functional-Analytic Course Design and the Variable Focus Curriculum" in *ELT Documents 124,* 10.
51. H.H. Stern, R. Vumann *et al. Module Making: A Study in the Development and Evaluation of Learning Materials for French as a Second Language.* Toronto: Ontario Ministry of Education, 1980, 60.
52. J.P.B. Allen. "General Purpose Language Teaching: A Variable Focus Approach." in *ELT Documents* 118, 69.
53. T. Hutchinson and A. Waters. *English For Specific Purposes.* Cambridge: Cambridge University Press, 1987, 107.
54. G. Brown and G. Yule. *Teaching the Spoken Language.* Cambridge: Cambridge University Press, 1983, 83.
55. Hutchinson and Waters. 1987, 122.
56. Hutchinson and Waters. 1987, 110.
57. W.M. Rivers and B.J. Melvin. "Language Learners as Individuals: Discovering their Needs, Wants and Learning Styles" in J.E. Alatis, H.B. Altman and P.M. Alatis (eds.). *The Second Language Classroom Directions for the 1980s,* Oxford: Oxford University Press, 1981.
58. A Little John. "Learner-Choice in Language Study." *ELT Journal* 39: 253-61.
59. Tom Hutchinson. "What's Underneath? An Interactive View of Materials Evaluation in Leisure" in E. Sheldon (ed.). *ELT Textbooks and Materials: Problems in Evaluating and Development. ELT Documents* 126. 1987, 37.
60. Alan Cunningsworth. *Evaluating and Selecting EFL Teaching Materials.* 57.
61. A. Brink *et al. Let's Try To Do it Better.* Adelaide, South Australian Adult Migrant Education Service, 1985, 9.
62. G. Brindley. *Needs Analysis and Objective Setting in the Adult Migration Education Program,* Sydney. NSW Adult Migrant Education Service,1984, 111.
63. R.L. Allwright. "Making Sense of Instruction: Whats the Problem"? Papers in *Applied Linguistics.* PALM: University of Michigan, (2): 1-10. 2.
64. Ian Tudor, *Learner-Centredness as Language Education,* 62.
65. Ian Tudor, 64.
66. J.Van E.K and J.L.M. Trim. *Across The Threshold.* Pergamon Press: Council of Europe, 1984, 23.
67. M.H. Long and G. Crookes. "Intervention Points in Second Language Classroom Processed." Paper presented at the *RELC Seminar,* Singapore, 21-26 April 1988.
68. M.H. Long and P.A. Porter. "Group-Work, Inter-Language Talk and Second Language Acquisition." *TESOL Quarterly* 19(2). 1985, 207-28.

69. S.D. Krashen. *Principles and Practice in Secondary Language Aquisition.* Oxford: Pergamon Press, 1982.
70. Swain. 1985.
71. E.Various and S. Gass. "Target Language Input from Non-Native Speakers". Paper presented at the Seventeenth Annual *TESOL Convention*, Toronto, 1983.
72. Quoted in J.T. Roberts. "The Use of Dialogues for Teaching Transactional Competence in Foreign Language" in *ELT Documents* 12, 57.
73. J. Revell. *Teaching Techniques for Communicative English.*
74. J. Revell. *Teaching Techniques for Communicative English.* 61.
75. J. Revell. *Teaching Techniques for Communicative English.* 62.
76. J. Rath. "Teaching without Specific Objectives" in L. Stenhouse. *An Introduction to Curriculum Research and Development.* London: Heinemann, 1975, 86-7.
77. Jane Revell. *Teaching Techniques for Communicative English.* London: Macmillan Publishers, 1979, 10-11.
78. J. Revell. *Teaching Techniques for Communicative English.* 11.
79. M.P. Breen and C.N. Candlin. "The Essentials of a Communicative Curriculum in Language Teaching." *Applied Linguistics* 2,1. 1980, 89-112.
80. Alan Maley. "A Rose is a Rose or Is It: Can Communicative Competence be Taught" in C.J. Brumfit (ed.). *The Practice of Communicative Teaching.* London: The British Council and Pergamon Press, 1986, 89.
81. N.S. Prabhu. *Second Language Pedagogy.* 4.
82. Paulston, 1971.
83. W.M. Rivers. "The Foreign Language Teachers and Cognitive Psychology or Where Do We Go from Here?" in Rivers, 1976: 109-30.
84. W. Littlewood. *Communicative Language Teaching: An Introduction.* Cambridge University Press, 1981.
85. C. Brumfit. *Communicative Methodology in Language Teaching. The Roles of Fluency and Accuracy,* 1984.
86. R. Oxford and M. Ehrman. "Second Language Research on Individual Differences" in *Annual Review of Applied linguistics* 13, 188-205.
87. J.Van EK and J.L.M. Trim. *Across the Threshold,* 149.
88. Quoted in J.Van EK and J.L.M. Trim. *Across the Threshold,* 171.
89. How this will be done in our local situation is discussed in Chapter 4.
90. W. Rivers. "From Linguistic Competence to Communicative Competence." in *TESOL* Vol. 7, No. 1, 1973, 28.
91. W.R. Rivers. "From Linguistic Competence to Communicative Competence" in *TESOL* Vol. 7, No. 1, 1973, 28.
92. W.R. Rivers. 1973, 28.
93. Trim. 1976, 78.

94. Testing or assessment is made towards the end of a course to find out what the learner has learnt. It has therefore, limited perspective with a focus on the product of learning while evaluation focuses on the means and is intended to serve the learning process.

95. Evaluation that focuses on monitoring the ongoing development of a course is known as formative evaluation. Such an evaluation involves getting information/feedback about the various aspects of the programme during the course itself. Summative evaluation focuses on the overall outcome, i.e. the end product of a programme which usually tends to involve tests and measurements. Information from summative evaluation is usually used to decide whether students have passed the course or not, as in our final exams.

96. R. Leblanc and G. Painchand. "Self-Assessment as a Second Language Placement Instrument" in *TESOL Quarterly* 1985, 673-87.

97. Ian Tudor. *Learner-Centredness as Language Education*. 167.

98 J.Van EK and J.L.M. Trim. *Across The Threshold*. 154.

99. J.Van EK and J.L.M. Trim. *Across The Threshold*. 154.

100. Ian Tudor. *Learner-Centredness as Language Education*. 252.

101. H. Holec. *Autonomy and Foreign Language Learning*. Strasbourg: Council of Europe.1979, 27.

102. A. Wenden. "What Do Second Language Learners Know About Their Language Learning? A Second Look at Retrospective Accounts." *Applied Linguistics* 7, 186-205.

103. F. Dubin and E. Olshtain. *Course Design: Developing Programmes and Materials for Language Learning*. Cambridge: Cambridge University Press. 1986, 79-80.

104. H. Holec. *Autonomy and Foreign Language Learning*, 27.

105. J.L.M. Trim. *Developing A Unit/Credit Scheme of Adult Language Learning*. Oxford: Pergamon Press, 1980, 7.

106. G. Brindley. *Needs Analysis and Objective Setting in the Adult Migrant Education Program*. 97.

107. D. Nunan. *The Learner-Centred Curriculum*. Cambridge: Cambridge University Press, 1988, 77.

108. Alen Maley. "A Rose Is a Rose or Is It?: Can Communicative Competence Be Taught?" in C.J. Brumfit, 1986, 95.

109. Ian Tudor. *Learner-Centredness as Language Education*. 252.

110. J. Wagner. "Innovation in Foreign Language Teaching" *AILA Review 5*, 99-117.

111. N.S. Prabhu. *Second Language Pedagogy*. 105.

112. J.Van EK and J.L.M.Trim. *Across the Threshold*. 17.

113. Luk Prodoromon."The Good Language Teacher" *English Teaching Forum* 29, 2: 1991, 2-7.

114. Jeremy Harmer. *The Practice of English Language Teaching*. Longman Series. 1983, 201.
115. S. Gaies and R. Bowers. "Clinical supervision of language teaching: The supervisor as trainer and educator" in J.C. Richards and D. Nunan. *Second Language Teacher Education*. Cambridge: Cambridge University Press, 1990, 95.
116. That this is practical, has been borne out by the Panjab University and the Delhi University where an effective syllabus has been framed along communicative lines.
117. K.M. Willey. "Language Games" in W.R. Lee (ed.). *E.L.T. Selections 2: Articles from English Language Teaching*. London: Oxford University Press, 1967, 95.
118. *Ibid.*, 95.
119. Ian Tudor. *Learner-Centredness as Language Education*. 140.
120. Ian Tudor. 252.
121. A. Wenden. *Learner Strategies for Learner Autonomy*. Hemel Hempstead. Prentice Hall, 1991, 7.
122. S.C. Sood. *New Directions in English Language and Literature Teaching in India*. Ajanta Publications, 1988, 108.
123. S.C. Sood, 108.
124. University Grants Commission. *Report of Curriculum Development Centre in English*, New Delhi, UGC, 1989, 328.
125. Alan Maley. "A Rose Is a Rose or Is It: Can Communicative Competence Be Taught?" in C.J. Brumfit. 1986, 96.
126. Pushpinder Syal. "The New Syllabus in Communication Skills in Punjab University and the Role of ELT Centre" *Focus on English*, 6, 1: 1990, 19-24.
127. Alan Tonkyn. "Observations on Syllabus Reform" *Focus on English*, 4, 3: 1988, 21-27.

3

The Present Indian Scenario: An Analysis of the Data Collected

In spite of teaching English to our students for quite sometime now (since independence), we still find that they lack the ability, both to communicate and to express their ideas in English. The reasons seem to be manifold. Firstly and primarily, it is the faulty syllabus and the faulty classroom procedures used; secondly, it is the wrong choice of the materials used, and, thirdly, the teachers have miserably failed to respond to the changing circumstances in our country and to the recent development in the field of language teaching. The Boards of Studies in most of our universities have totally refused to understand the needs of the second language learner.[1] We have not clearly formulated the realistic objectives of teaching English. Even if we have spelt the aims, we have not clearly thought of evaluating the realization of these aims. Hence the appalling standards of English.

English language teaching involves devising of teaching methods, designing of syllabuses, preparing teaching materials and other pedagogic factors that lie at the heart of a teaching programme. I shall discuss each of these components in detail with respect to the specific position in Kashmir. What is true of Kashmir is true of any other Indian State. Though the Syllabus content varies from State to State yet the methodology, the techniques used and the overall aims and objectives of the curriculum are the same throughout.

Let us take the first factor, i.e. the teaching method into consideration. At present we seem to be using an eclectic method taking some components from the Grammar-Translation Method and a few from the Direct Method. Like the Grammar-Translation Method we focus on the reading and writing skills and pay little or no systematic attention to speaking and listening. Grammar is taught deductively, that is, by presentation and study of grammar rules, and accuracy is emphasized and errors are corrected at once. Translation is used in the classroom as a technique to make the difficult words understood but is not used as a method. It is used as a skill and forms a component of grammar; but since translation is not used as a mode in teaching language skills or in teaching grammar so we cannot be said to be using the Grammar-Translation Method altogether; but since translation is used as a technique we cannot be said to conform to the Direct Method either.

Our present method has not helped our students to develop their language skills. Speaking and writing suffer most. Reading and listening though developed to a certain extent, are not satisfactory. The reason for this is quite obvious. We are ignoring the speaking skill altogether. "To speak any language," as Dr. Ballard observes, "whether native or foreign, entirely by rule is quite impossible."[2] Unless we actually make our students speak in the class and provide them with rich language input, nothing positive is going to take place. E.C. Kittson supports this view by saying, "learning to speak a language is always by far the shortest road to learning to read it and to write it.... By using the language as speech, the pupil will cover something like twenty times as much ground in a given time as he would by doing written exercises.... The acquiring of a language is the acquiring of the art, the art of expressing oneself in that language; this art like every other art must be acquired by practice, that is by using the language, the most satisfactory manner of using the language from the practical point of view of economy of time and effort is as speech, and it is also theoretically the most natural; it follows therefore, that a language should be learnt by speaking it."[3]

Our lecture method does not give the student any chance of speaking his mind. Although the teacher desperately wants the students to respond yet she is limited by the constraints of lengthy syllabus, limited time and unmanageable classroll. As a result, teaching has become what Verma remarks, "a unidirectional process of pumping bits and pieces of unrelated and undigested goblets of knowledge into empty sacks."[4] On the other hand learning is a bidirectional interactional process where the learners give as much as they receive. The learning process should help learners to exploit their hidden talent.

Our present method lays great stress on the deductive use of grammar. The fault, however, as Catford remarks, "is not that it (the Grammar-Translation Method) uses grammar and translation but that it uses them badly."[5] Menon[6] is of the view, "grammar is an essential part of the whole English course but it should not be regarded as a separate subject implying that it should be taught inductively as it comes in the texts prescribed for general English."

Presently we have a separate book for teaching English grammar and though it is labelled "communicative skills,' speaking and listening skills are altogether ignored. The grammar exercises are content-bound and do not help our students to move from the level of context-governed performance to that of context-free competence. As Verma rightly believes, "it is not enough to have our pupils perform well in doing simple context-bound exercises. They must be helped to use the language in non-classroom situations communicating with a variety of speakers in a variety of contexts."[7] Sah feels that the inability of our students to communicate in real life situations "leads to a situation in which one of the important purposes of retaining English in India, *viz.* to serve as a lingua franca among educated people is not realized in full."[8]

Another crucial aspect is the use of translation in teaching. Since the textbooks framed for our degree classes are much beyond their comprehension (as far as language and content are concerned) we (teachers) have to resort to the use of the mother tongue or the second language in order to get the meaning across. The whole classroom activity seems to be a mere paraphrasing of difficult words and getting the meaning (of the text) across the students. The use of the mother tongue is useful but too much use of it defeats the very purpose of teaching English. Moreover, it minimizes the exposure to the language which is vital for providing the necessary comprehensible input to our students. Dr. Jean Forrester allows the use of the mother tongue in two situations—first, "when there is no English equivalent known to the pupils since it is useless to explain a difficult word by giving a more difficult English equivalent. Second, when the use will save time."[9] Menon and Patel are of the view that the teacher should avoid any possibility of giving his pupils a feeling of hopelessness, defeat and discouragement. If translation helps he should use it; if it is likely to lead to mistakes, he should avoid it. If translation has to be used, the teacher should use it and quickly get back into English.[10]

Our present situation makes extensive use of translation in order to make the texts comprehensible. It however, has a negative impact as well. Too much translation deprives our students of a language-rich environment which is so vital for language acquisition. It impoverishes them by reducing their language input. Mary Jane in her article 'Linguistic Science and its Classroom Reflections" talks of "uniqueness of each language (which) makes most word-for-word translation invalid and suggests that translation is not a good device....[11] I personally feel that in our present situation where the proficiency of our students is at variance with the degree of complexity of our prescribed texts, the teacher is hard-pressed to use translation, the avoidance of which would lead to a total lack of comprehension on the part of the learner. In our situation, therefore, translation is unavoidable. The best thing to do would be to use it and quickly get back into English. In order to avoid too much use of translation, I would suggest textbooks which are only slightly above their comprehension."

Taking the second major factor in English Language Teaching, i.e. the syllabus into consideration. We find a wide gap between what should be and what actually is. Let us go into the details and see where we have gone wrong.

Corder believes that an ideal syllabus should help the teacher to understand:

- What he is expected to teach and in what order?
- What educational purpose is his teaching to serve?
- What teaching methods are known to achieve these purposes?
- What standards of achievement is he expected to aim at?
- How will he receive the feedback?
- What can be usefully told about the competence interests and attitudes of the students he is to teach?[12]

These questions imply that the teacher looks for a thorough guidance in the syllabus regarding (1) aims and objectives (2) contents (3) methods (4) evaluation and (5) learner's characteristics. In other words, the syllabus should contain all the information that the teacher needs to implement and execute the teaching programme that has been handed down to her by the authorities. She may, however, modify or reformulate the aims in accordance with his classroom situation, students' abilities and the time allotted to her.

Every syllabus should specify the aims and objectives. Jain has rightly said that it is the objectives that determine the method.[13] Koul talks of the aims and objectives of teaching English at the primary, middle and higher level at school. He talks of developing the four basic language skills laying more emphasis on listening and speaking at the primary level. "The teacher must supervise and correct pronunciation including stress and intonation."[14] At level II the emphasis on spoken English should continue. There must be emphasis on the practical use of the language rather than a discussion of it. "The students should be encouraged to adapt text-conversations to real situations as far as possible and try to personalise them."[15] At level III the main aim should be to develop oral competence in speaking English with fluency and accuracy in day to day actual situation.[16]

The framing of aims and objectives "is influenced by two major considerations: (1) needs (2) resources available. Needs will refer to the social and individual needs; the resources available will refer to the (a) teachers available and their linguistic competence (b) time available within the curriculum (c) and the equipment the teacher will need to teach the language."[17] The syllabus as a guide will then justify those aims in terms of social and educational contexts. It will justify why it aims to develop the skills it specifies. The syllabus should contain information about what kind of teaching should go in the classroom. It should make provision for the teacher to plan the classroom teaching in such a way that the teaching items receive adequate attention in the class. The syllabus will also identify the skills that would be required. It will also mention the priorities that the teacher would give to these skills. Thus we see that the syllabus is a complete comprehensive guide both to the teacher and the students. For the teacher it contains everything that she needs to organise her classroom teaching, choose her methods and plan the course for the year. For the students it is the goal and the end-product. The syllabus should be an agreed framework of a programme between the teacher and her pupils. While framing the syllabus the teacher should be taken into consideration. He/she in turn will take the students' interests and needs into consideration since he/she is the best judge of what will suit his/her students. The teacher, the head of the institution, the university authorities, the board of education, the curriculum specialist, the curriculum advisor, all should jointly frame the syllabus in a comprehensive, integrated and well co-ordinated way. Koul is of the opinion that it would be ideal to entrust the test of the preparation of a language curriculum to a central professional agency whose function is mandatory and not just advisory.[18]

Looking at our present syllabuses we find that they are inadequate as well as disoriented. Our present syllabuses make learners learn everything without knowing or feeling it from their life situations' point of view. The students find the life situations and the course contents quite unrelated. Our unrealistic syllabuses are examination-oriented. They are finished and learned for the examinations. Both the students and the teachers feel that passing of the examination is the only aim of learning the language. An examination-based syllabus is bound to produce students with low proficiency and the materials selected for the purpose also conform to this scheme. Hutchinson and Waters[19] have labelled five kinds of syllabuses—evaluation syllabus, organisational syllabus, material syllabus, classroom syllabus and learner syllabus. Our syllabuses at present are a mixture of several types of syllabuses. They are evaluation syllabuses, i.e. a kind of syllabus handed down by ministries which states what the successful learner will know by the end of the course. In effect it puts on record the basis on which success or failure will be evaluated as well as listing what should be learnt. Our syllabuses also state the order in which it is to be learnt. They are also, therefore, organisational syllabuses. The organisational syllabus bases contents on the nature of language and of learning, e.g. easier things to be learnt first. These two syllabuses are regarded as pure syllabuses since they are not listed. They are external since the learner does not participate in their creation in any way.[20] Our present syllabuses can also be labelled as grammatical since the syllabus content is selected and graded according to grammatical notions of simplicity and complexity. Let me explain these points from the situation in the Kashmir region which is typical of the Indian situation. The general English syllabus presented for B.A. Part I of Three Year Degree Course (in operation since 1999) has the following format:

PAPER A

Essays and Stories

Text Twentieth Century English Prose (OUP)

Selected Modern Stories K.G. Seshadir (ed.) (Macmillan)

Earnest Hemingway: *The Old Man and the Sea*

Examination Pattern

The question paper will consist of five questions:

Q.No. 1. Four passages for explanation with reference to the context from Twentieth Century English Prose. Out of these, the students will be required to attempt two. However, no passages will be set from the following: "The Night the Ghost Got In," "Bores," "The First Five Minutes" and "Mohan the Man-Eater." (15 marks)

Q.No. 2. One essay type question with an alternative from text 1. (15 marks)

Q.No. 3. One essay type question with an alternative from text 2. (15 marks)

Q.No. 4. One essay type question with an alternative from text 3. (15 marks)

Q.No. 5. One essay type question from text 2 with an alternative from text 3. (15 marks)

PAPER B

Communication Skills

1. Paragraph writing
2. Informal letter writing
3. Tenses
4. (a) Direct and indirect speech
   (b) The articles
5. Translation of a Kashmiri/Urdu/Hindi/ Punjabi passage into English.

The paper will consist of five questions:

Q.No. 1. A paragraph to be developed from any one of the five given topic sentences. (20 marks)

Q.No. 2. (a) One question relating to the use of verbs.
(b) One question relating to the tenses.
(5+5 marks)

Q.No. 3. An informal letter with an alternative. (15 marks)

Q.No. 4. (a) A short passage relating to the change of narration.
(b) A short passage with gaps to be filled in with the articles. (10+5 marks)

Q.No. 5. Translation of a non-idiomatic Hindi/Urdu/Kashmiri/ Punjabi passage into English. (15 marks)

Suggested Books

1. *Communication Skills-1,* Mohammad Aslam, Srinagar; KBD.
2. *Essentials of English Grammar,* Richard Murphey, Cambridge University Press.

It is evident that the syllabus only states the marks allocated to prescribed texts and the texts that are prescribed for detailed and non-detailed study. The rest is left to the teacher to decide.

The syllabus is ambiguous and inadequate in every respect. It does not say what skills the teacher should develop in students; what activities should be adopted to teach the syllabus; how much time should be spent on each topic; how the teacher should go about teaching the four skills; which skills should be given more emphasis, etc. In fact the syllabus doesn't even touch these aspects. Everything is left to the teacher to decide on her own whether it matches with the planners' objectives or not.

The syllabus for B.A. Part I of the Three Year Degree Course prescribes a textbook for Paper A which contains essays of various kinds—sports, description, education, etc. Textbooks of these sorts do not in any way improve the language skills of the learner. The students are like mute spectators watching the teacher lecture in front of them. Comprehensive questions when asked reveal that the majority of the students are not grasping the idea that is being taught. The condition seems at times hopeless. There is no mention in the syllabus as to which method of teaching has to be employed with the result that the textbook lends itself to varied interpretation and methods. Further, the syllabus fails to contain guidelines for the students (or the teacher) as to how to use the book. The information contained in the syllabus could help the paper setter but not the student or the teacher. An ideal situation would have been to provide an appropriate and suitable guide—in the form of a teachers' book for the teacher and the student.

The syllabus is content-oriented rather than skill-oriented. As Sah rightly believes that in our schools and colleges we teach English as a content subject and not a language subject.[21] Sah believes that it would be advisable to set out the language syllabus (for schools and colleges) in greater detail in terms of skills and abilities expected of the pupils at every level and to specify the ways teachers are expected to go about realizing this syllabus apart from the use of the textbooks, dependence on which should be minimized as much as possible. Examples of detailed specification for English are: ability to greet in English, ask questions about the addressee's health and welfare, ask questions about the time and places of actions and events, seek and give directions for places, make inquiries about persons, arrangements, etc. A syllabus set out in this way will provide little scope for confusion with the textbook and will lead the teacher to rely mainly upon her own resources. Instead, our syllabus is content-based. Shakespeare, Keats, Milton and other literary figures find a place in the course (in the General English course of IInd year degree class) though the student fails to make the 'subject-verb' distinction. No attention is given to the central purpose of General English—developing the language skills. Baneriji has rightly remarked:

> The GE syllabus at present seems to fulfil merely an administrative requirement. It is there because it has to be. Appalling irrelevance and lack of purpose characterize it and this is a sad commentary on the educational planning of a country which has made significant progress in many other fields of knowledge and activity.[22]

Our students who are supposed to read poetry (in IInd Year Degree Course) can hardly write a grammatically correct sentence or can hardly express themselves in English. It would be better if we taught them language skills especially the speaking skill rather than teaching them poetry. Lado rightly believes, "conversational dialogues are preferable to poetry or formal prose because conversation shows a greater range of the basic construction of the language in matter-of-fact context."[23] Lado further states, "one cannot jump from the structure of a language into its literature without passing through the cultural content of the language. Careful selection of contextual areas for the dialogue and reading material permits full use of the language in limited areas early in the course. Pictures, slides or a film may help significantly to provide cultural content for observations by the students."[24]

One major drawback in our syllabus is that it ignores the learner altogether. The learner should form an essential component of the teaching process, because without his active participation, any teaching programme is bound to produce least results. For any individual to learn a language, whether it is his mother tongue or any other language, three things must be present in a positive degree, i.e. aptitude, motivation and opportunity.

Our existing system takes none of these crucial elements into account. Neither does our system see the aptitude of our learners, nor do we concern ourselves about whether they are ready to learn, nor do we provide them with opportunities to use the language in such a way as will be relevant to them in their everyday life.

Moreover, our syllabuses overlook the great heterogeneity in the levels of the achievement of students. Students from different educational backgrounds with varying levels of achievement are all grouped together. The proficiency level of our students varies greatly from student to student. This is mainly due to the varied level of English our students are exposed to in their schools. The exposure they get varies from 2 years to 15 years, depending upon the type of school they have attended. Added to this varied exposure to English at the school level is the varied socio-economic background of our pupils. We have now been getting more and more students from the lower strata of society and from rural areas. They are first generation students with poor learning environments. There is none at home, competent enough to guide them in their studies and they do not have the resources to hire one. They also lack modern technological means such as TV, DVD, computers, etc. which positively affect the child's personality and his communicative skills. Many of them are unable to buy even the prescribed textbooks not to say of buying extra reading materials. Moreover, these students have very little time to devote to their studies as they have to help their parents in the fields or at their homes. Above all, they are from regional medium schools in the rural areas with hardly any language teaching/learning facility. Our students, therefore, differ not only in their exposure to English but also in their socio-economic backgrounds. In fact, Sood has rightly pointed out that excepting age (18+) sex (both male and female) and nationality (Indian) there is hardly anything else in common among these groups.[25]

The result of such grouping is detrimental to the interests of the bright students as well to the dull students. While the bright students get bored by repetition and lose their motivation, the dull students want continuous repetition and drilling. The grouping of such students is, therefore, disastrous for them both.

The third factor (in English Language Teaching) is the teaching material used. Our teaching material is neither purposeful and need-based, nor interesting and motivating. Our textbooks have so far been selected without any prior thought about the suitability and authenticity of their language and content. They are not written with a definite aim in view. One finds a big gap between the language used in these texts and the needs of the students who use these textbooks. Srivendra Verma suggests that we should choose and select textbooks "...on the basis of *our* needs, *our* problems and limitations and the socio-cultural settings in which *we* are learning and teaching English (emphasis mine)."[26] Our prescribed textbooks are not suitably edited for foreign learners/ teachers. Widdowson describes the principles of evaluating and selecting authentic texts for communicative language teaching. He believes that the authenticity of materials depends not only on the matic appropriacy but also on its style (i.e., who wrote it for whom):

> The material written by a scientist in a professional journal would differ if he were writing the same material in a school textbook for a group of students or if he were writing it for a popular daily. The problem is to edit our materials in such a way as to guide the learners to an

awareness of the communicative conventions operating in the kind of discourse they will be concerned in real life.[27]

Our instructional materials are often selected by the Boards of Studies (at the undergraduate and postgraduate levels) and by the Boards of School Education at the school level. Although teachers are represented on these boards, their selection is made on seniority basis. A few representatives from a large population of teachers often results in decisions which, more often than not, are relunctantly accepted by the remaining teachers. Also the senior teachers who become the members of these Boards neither possess the necessary expertise and knowledge of writing and developing materials nor feel motivated to allow any radical changes even if a large number of teachers as well as students feel totally dissatisfied with the existing materials. Naturally, the selection is made from the commercially available textbooks which the Indian publishers produce for no obvious purposes and no particular learning aims and objectives in view. This dependence on the available textbooks makes the teachers and students adhere to either the exercises given at the end of the texts or in the absence of these exercises rely on student guides (which are known as Bazaar Notes). These 'Bazaar Notes' get authenticity once the examination papers are based on them (and that very often happens).

Our textbooks have no positive aim to teach language use in real-life situations. They do not take the reader beyond the ideas that the writer wants to convey. The exercises at the end are mostly textual, on the theme, on subject matter, etc., of a particular passage. Any attempt to teach language as such, if at all made, is confined to the teaching of linguistic items and other grammatical forms, for instance 'direct and indirect speech', etc. The textbooks that belong to the literary genres like Drama, Novel, etc., (however high they may be in their style and theme) do not equip the students with the communicative skills that he needs in interacting in real-life situations. Neither Thomas Hardy nor Haldane can become a model for language use in social interactions.

In selecting texts for our students, we have to, moreover, decide about the extent and kind of cultural exposure that would be desirable for our students. Should we expose them to the Indian culture or to some western and alien culture or to some world culture? In making our selection we have to see that the cultural content that is sought to be taught through the textbooks should be oriented to cater to the needs of the students who are born and brought up in the Indian cultural milieu. We can possibly include those things which will enhance the student's vision of the diversity of Indian culture. Such elements of culture should be given priority as are known to the students. Sareen believes that anything that is too unfamiliar, remote or too incongruent may baffle and bemuse the learner rather than aid learning.[28]

Halliday believes that if the cultural items in our textbooks are too remote they "might provide a cultural shock and impede the learning process...."[29]

Keeping these aspects in view let us look at length at the syllabus of B.Sc. Part II and B.Sc. Part III of the Three Year Degree Course for General English (in operation since 1999). For B.Sc. Part II we have the following format:

Paper A

The following texts are prescribed:

(1) *A Choice of Poems* (Macmillan)

(2) *Six Famous Plays* (Ed. S. Single)

(3) *A Selection of English Prose* (Orient Longman)

Only the following poems are prescribed:

Sonnet L	Shakespeare
Sonnet XVII (On His Blindness)	John Milton
London	William Blake
Resolution and Independence	William Wordsworth
Song to the Men of England	P.B. Shelley
La Belle Dame Sans Merci	John Keats
Dover Beach	Matthew Arnold
Adam's Curse	W.B. Yeats
The Unknown Citizen	W.H. Auden

Examination Pattern

Q.No. 1. One compulsory question on explanation with reference to the context from *A Choice of Poems*, three out of six passages to be attempted. (15 marks)

Q.No. 2. One question with an alternative from *A Choice of Poems*.

Q.No. 3. One question with an alternative on *Six Famous Plays*. (15 marks)

Q.No. 4. One question with an alternative on *A Selection of English Prose*. (15 marks)

Q.No. 5. One question on *Six Famous Plays* with an alternative on *A Selection of English Prose*.

PAPER B

Communicative Skills-II

(1) Formal letter writing

(2) Comprehension passages with questions

(3) Vocabulary testing

(a) Spelling

(b) Use of idioms and phrases into sentences

(c) Use of a word as different parts of speech

(4) Translation of a passage from Urdu/Hindi/ Kashmiri/ Punjabi into English

Examination Pattern

Q.No. 1. The candidates will be asked to write a formal letter out of two choices. (20 marks)

Q.No. 2. A comprehensive passage followed by questions. (15 marks)

Q.No. 3. (a) One question on correct spelling. (5 marks)

(b) One question on idioms and phrases. (5 marks)

(c) One question on the use of a word as different parts of speech. (5 marks)

Q.No. 4. (a) Five sentences involving the use of prepositions. (15 marks)

(b) Five sentences involving the correct use of articles. (5 marks)

Q.No. 5. A passage in Urdu/Hindi/Kashmiri/Punjabi to be translated into English. (15 marks)

Suggested Books

(1) *Communication Skills-II* Mohammad Aslam Srinagar; KBD.

(2) *Written Communication in English* Sarah Freeman, Orient Longman.

Looking at the syllabus of B.Sc. Part II we find that the texts are literature-based. We are teaching our students language through literature. All the three texts are different forms of literature (poems, plays and prose). The irony is that while our students find it hard to form a grammatically correct sentence, we are thrusting works of literature down their throat. What justice they can do to these texts and how much they will be benefited by them is quite obvious. The whole syllabus seems absurd and meaningless. Literature and especially the kind prescribed for our degree classes is as Rodger believes, such that it "...itself presupposes by its very nature a command of the language so complete that it forms the background against which the reader interprets the writers' deliberate and significant deviations...."[30] He further adds "...(it) can mean nothing to a student who is unable to construe the text and so discover what its meaning potential is."[31] This is exactly the case with our students. The prescribed literature means 'nothing to them' since they are 'unable to construe the text.' Literature shall not be ignored. It shall assume its due place in the later years and can be taken up as an optional subject at the higher level. Jain has rightly pointed out that since "much emphasis is laid upon the linguistic exercises...the aim and purpose of teaching a piece of literature is defeated.... Similarly, the teaching of a short story or a one-act play or a drama is not possible through methods of teaching which lay much emphasis upon linguistic aspects."[32] Rodger, therefore, suggests, "that the selection of the material for study be made on (i) linguistic rather than aesthetic grounds and (ii) teachability of the material...."[33] Widdowson[34] also agrees that we should move from stylistically simple material to more complex one.

At present there is a wide gap between the proficiency level of our college students and the proficiency demands of our texts. The two are incompatible. This is again evident when we consider the syllabus of B.Sc. Part III of the Three Year Degree Course for General English (in operation since 1999). We find the following format:

PAPER A

Following texts are prescribed:

Arthur Miller : *All My Sons*

P.G. Wodehouse : *The Inimitable Jeeves*

Enlightenment : *A Selection of Essays for Awareness*

Examination Pattern

Q.No. 1. One compulsory question on explanation with reference to the context from *All My Sons*. Three out of six passages to be attempted. (15 marks)

Q.No. 2. One question with an alternative on *All My Sons*.

Q.No. 3. One question with an alternative on *The Inimitable Jeeves*. (15 marks)

Q.No. 4. One question with an alternative on *Enlightenment*. (15 marks)

Q.No. 5. One question from *The Inimitable Jeeves* with an alternative on *Enlightenment*. (15 marks)

PAPER B

Q.No. 1. Essays out of five given topics. Candidates to attempt one. (25 marks)

Q.No. 2. Precis writing (15 marks)

Q.No. 3. Applied Grammar

(a) Pairs of words (4 marks)

(b) Modal verbs (4 marks)

(c) A passage for change of narration (8 marks)

(d) Prepositional phrases (4 marks)

Q.No. 4. Translation from Hindi/Urdu/Punjabi into English. (15 marks)

Books Recommended

Sara Freeman : *Written Communication in English;* Orient Longman

Mohammad Aslam : *Communication Skills - III*

Paper A, as we have seen, consists of works of literature and we are again teaching language through literature. The problems are the same as discussed. These works of art in no way help our students to use language efficiently and effectively. As Lado rightly believes, "to know a language is to use its pattern of construction with appropriate vocabulary at normal speed for communication."[35]

Our students lack this ability (to use language) and our syllabus and the textbooks used, add to this inability to communicate. Gatenby is of the opinion that:

> One of the greatest faults we make in our present system of education is the attempt to teach a second language as if it were an ordinary school subject like history, geography, literature or science, all of which can be learnt by listening to a teacher....[36]

What we have to keep in mind as language teachers is that exposure to a rich variety of linguistic and socio-cultural material with its focus on 'what to say when and how' is of paramount importance in second language learning.

The most challenging problem for the teacher to tackle is the one arising out of students' incompetence in handling written English. Aslam rightly points out that their English is neither acceptable nor correct.... They fail to write correct English not only at the sentence level but also at the discourse level.[37]

One of the reasons for this incompetence could be the passive attitudes which the present method implies on the learner. The learner is not actively involved in the classroom activity. The classroom activity remains a teacher-dominated exercise giving lectures for forty-five minutes (which includes the taking of attendance) explaining the meanings of difficult words and phrases, preparing students for examinations and finishing the course within the stipulated time, is all that our existing classroom teaching means. There is very little interaction between the teacher and the students or among the students to ensure the promotion of communicative skills. The whole classroom activity seems to be a futile exercise with the teacher desperately trying to thrust the prescribed material upon the students without having any time left for assessing the assimilation of these ideas by the students. The time factor is a very restricting factor. If we consider the syllabus of B.Sc. Part I of the Three Year Degree Course in General English, we find that we have to cover three texts. *Twentieth Century Prose* has twelve essays out of which eight are for detailed study from which questions of reference to passages are asked in the examination. In addition, there are twelve short stories to be taught from the selected short stories.[38] In addition, we have a novel—*The Old Man and the Sea.* Besides, we have to teach grammar. All this has to be covered in the short span of six months with a calculated 16 hours time in one month (given 45 minutes per day and 6 days a week).[39] The problem of lengthy syllabus gets aggravated by the overcrowded classes which extend to even more than 100 students in a class when ideally the roll should have been not more than thirty five. In the short span of 45 minutes, it takes 15 minutes to mark the attendance reducing the time for actual teaching by almost half. As such, the syllabus becomes a burden for the teacher more than for the student. The teacher, no matter how efficient he/she is, is pulled down by these circumstances and cannot do justice to his/her job.

In an extensive survey carried out by this researcher in the Kashmir Valley, some fifteen colleges were surveyed. They are:

1. Govt. Degree College for Boys, Bemina, Kashmir, J&K.
2. Amar Singh College for Boys, Kashmir, J&K.
3. Islamia College for Boys, Kashmir, J&K.
4. Women's College M.A. Road, Kashmir, J&K.
5. Women's College, Nawakadal, Kashmir, J&K.

6. College for Education, Kashmir, J&K.
7. Govt. Degree College for Boys, Baramulla, Kashmir, J&K.
8. Govt. Degree College for Girls, Anantnag, Kashmir, J&K.
9. Govt. Degree College for Boys, Anantnag, Kashmir, J&K.
10. Govt. Degree College for Girls, Sopore, Kashmir, J&K.
11. Khalsa College Amritsar, Punjab.
12. Lady Sri Ram College, New Delhi.
13. Hindu College, New Delhi.
14. Women's College of Ranchi University, Jamshedpur, Jharkhand.
15. Government P.G. College Neemuch, Madhya Pradesh.

About 200 questionnaires were distributed—100 to teachers and 100 to students. The questionnaires for teachers were different from the questionnaires for students. These have been attached as Appendix A and Appendix B at the end. There were three columns for each question. There was a 'Yes' column, a 'No' column and a separate column for the comments of the students and the teachers. Sometimes the teachers and the students ticked just the 'Yes' or 'No' column without passing any comments. Sometimes the teachers and the students besides marking 'Yes' or 'No' gave their comments in the comment column. While tabulating the responses of the teachers and the students I have, therefore, made a separate column for those who passed their comments besides marking 'Yes' or 'No.' Those who did not comment at all and just marked 'Yes' or 'No' have also been listed in the 'Didn't Comment' column. The situation, though dealing with the J&K region, is applicable to the Indian scenario as a whole.

Looking at the present scenario, we find that all the aspects involved in language teaching are defective. The curriculum is framed by the ministries and handed down to the teacher. The aims and objectives are not clearly stated. The role of the teachers and that of the learners, the method to be used, the classroom techniques to be applied, are all ambiguous and dubious.

The syllabus, as both the teachers and learners feel, is too lengthy for all the three classes. It is not relevant to the needs of the students. Only the senior members of the teaching faculty are consulted while framing the syllabus and this has not in any way improved the contents either quantitatively or qualitatively. Moreover, our syllabuses are not listed. There is no instruction whatsoever, as to how to proceed, how much time to spend on each topic, which skills to be taught first.

The teaching materials used are not relevant to either their needs or their standards. They are difficult both as regards content and language. Moreover, they are not interesting. The responses given by the teachers clearly testify this:

- 73.4% of teachers feel that the materials used are greatly above their (students') level of comprehension.
- 70% of teachers feel the syllabus is uninteresting, demotivating and non-relevant to the needs of the students.
- 70% feel the syllabus does not teach all the four language skills.
- 90% feel that the syllabus does not contain clear guidance for the teacher as to how the material can be used to the best advantage of the student.
- 100% feel that they are handicapped due to lack of a teacher book.
- 93.4% feel that the syllabus does not provide a balance of activities appropriate for the students.
- 76.7% feel that materials used do not lead them into communication with each other.
- 93.4% feel that the materials used are not presented in realistic contexts.
- 86.7% are not in favour of continuing with these materials.

Regarding classroom procedures:

- 100% of teachers use the lecture mode with translation as the main technique.
- 93.3% feel that communicative and problem-solving activities should be introduced. Teachers are giving

clear preferences to communicative activities and to grammar (response No. 13 of teachers).

- 99% of teachers feel that the failure of our students to communicate is due to deficient schooling; lack of proper exposure to the language; late start for teaching English at school.
- 100% of teachers feel that the most grave problem facing them is unmanageable classroll, lengthy syllabus and limited time available.
- 100% of teachers feel that they are handicapped as far as using their own techniques in teaching the four skills are concerned.
- 89.5% of teachers prefer teaching in small groups.
- 70% of teachers feel that initially, language should be taught through language courses alone to improve the four skills.
- 76% of teachers are not in favour of continuing with the present method of teaching.

Regarding the method, teachers use a mixed method, using some features of Direct Method and some of the Grammar-Translation Method. They, however, find that this method is not helping their students to communicate.

From the present scenario (taking the responses of both the teachers and the students) it is obvious that the whole curriculum setting needs a revamping. Not only the aims and objectives need to be clearly defined but the syllabus, the materials used, the methods used, the techniques used in the class, the teacher's role, the learner's role, all need to be redefined. The responses of the teachers and more so of the students reveal that they are all set to face the challenges of the CLT, they are both prepared to accept the method (though they don't seem to be conscious of it). It is not only desirable at this juncture but is of prime necessity. If we want our teaching/learning to be productive we have to pay attention to several grave problems facing us at present.[40] A specially designed curriculum would be necessary so that our teaching and learning becomes effective and caters to the needs of our students. The curriculum should aim at specifying the objectives, relating these objectives to the needs of students, designing materials for achieving those objectives, and proposing effective and efficient teaching methods that would help to make learning easy and relevant to real life situations. These issues have been ignored so far and need a careful consideration if we wish to make our teaching and learning of English relevant to our needs. These and other related issues will be the topic of my discussion in the chapter that follows.

REFERENCES

1. This is a very crucial point which has been altogether ignored by our educational policy.
2. Quoted in T.K.N. Menon and M.S. Patel. *The Teaching of English as a Foreign language*. Baroda: Achriya Book Depot, 1957, 45.
3. Quoted in Menon and Patel. *The Teaching of English as a Foreign Language*. 75.
4. Shivendra K. Verma. "Teaching English as a Second Language in India," in Omkar N. Koul (ed.). *English in India: Theoretical and Applied Issues*. New Delhi: Creative Publishers, 1992, 225.
5. *Ibid.*
6. Menon & Patel. *The Teaching of English as a Foreign Language*. 89.
7. Shrivendra F. Verma. *Aspects of English Language Teaching*. 95.
8. Prajapati P. Sah. "Teaching English at the School Level: Some Observations" in Omkar N. Koul (ed.). *English in India*. 146.
9. Quoted in Menon & Patel. *The Teaching of English as a Foreign Language*. 88.
10. Menon & Patel. 91.
11. Mary Jane M. Morris. "Linguistic Science and its Classroom Reflections" in Harold B. Allen (ed.). *Applied English Linguistics*. Amerind Publishing. 1958, 350.
12. Pit Corder. *Introducing Applied Linguistics*. Penguin. 1973, 296.
13. R.K. Jain. *Essentials of English Teaching*. Vinod Pustak Mandira, 1985, 173.
14. Omkar N. Koul (ed.). *English in India: Theoretical and Applied Issues*. New Delhi: Creative Publishers. 1992, 244.
15. Omkar N. Koul (ed.). 1992, 245.
16. If Koul's aims and objectives are followed, many problems facing us at the college level will be solved.
17. Mohammad Aslam. *Trends in English Language Teaching in India*. Bareilly: PBD Publications. 1989.

18. Omkar N. Koul (ed.). *English in India*. 243.
19. Tom Hutchinson and Alan Waters. Cambridge: Cambridge University Press, 80-83.
20. Such syllabuses are concerned with the product rather than the process of learning. There is now a growing recognition that specification of the end products must also be accompanied by specifications of methodology.
21. Prajapati P. Sah. *op. ct.*, 146.
22. Banerji & Mohan. "General English Syllabuses: A Critical Review." *Journal of Higher Education* 10, 3:1985, 233-43.
23. Robert Lado. *Language Teaching: A Scientific Approach*. Bombay: Tata MacGraw Hill Publishing Co. Ltd., 51.
24. Lado. 151.
25. S.C. Sood. *New Directions in English Language and Literature Teaching in India*. Ajanta Publications, 1988, 23.
26. Shivendra K. Verma. *Aspects of English Language Teaching: Focus on Functions*. T.R. Publications, 1993, 115-116.
27. H.G. Widdowson. *Explorations in Applied Linguistics*. Oxford: Oxford University Press, 1979, 79.
28. S.R. Sareen. "Text Comprehensibility—the Socio-Culture Dimensions" in Omkar N. Koul (ed.). *English in India*, 234.
29. Quoted in Sareen, 234.
30. Alex Rodger. "Language for Literature" in C.T. Brumfit (ed.). *Teaching Literature Overseas: Language-based Approaches*. Pergamon, 1983, 87.
31. *Ibid.*, 87.
32. R.K. Jain. *Essentials of English Teaching*. Vinod Pustak Mandir, 1985, 172.
33. Alex Rodger. 1983, 88.
34. H.G. Widdowson. *Stylisties and the Teaching of Literature*. Longman 1975, 17.
35. Robert Lado. *Language Teaching: A Scientific Approach*. 50.
36. E.V. Gatenby. "Translation in the Classroom" in W.R. Lee (ed.). *E.L.T. Selections* 2. Oxford University Press, 1967, 69.
37. Mohammad Aslam. "Local Errors in the Use of English at the Undergraduate Level in Kashmir." *English Studies in India*. 1983: 101-109.
38. I personally find these stories dull, uninteresting and demotivating for the students.
39. The same is true of the lengthy syllabus of B.Sc. II and B.Sc. III of the Three Year Degree Course for General English.
40. The problems can be listed as:
    (i) Unmanageable class-roll

(ii) Limited time
(iii) Lengthy syllabus
(iv) Lack of proper planning
(v) Unspecified aims and objectives
(vi) Unrealistic materials
(vii) Outdated methods
(viii) Faulty testing techniques, and
(ix) Lack of feedback.

4

Implementation of the Communicative Method in our Situation

So far we have seen the drawback in our present system; the problem faced by us (as teachers) and the limitations and restrictions under which we have to work. We have also seen that some of the grave problems facing us at present are:

1. Unmanageable class-roll.
2. Heterogeneous learner groups with low motivational levels.
3. Undefined curriculum.
4. Unlisted, examination-oriented syllabuses.
5. Uninteresting classroom techniques.
6. Outdated learning strategies.
7. Untrained language teachers.

For the communicative method to be implemental, each problem has to be tackled and solutions have to be found. Let us discuss each problem along with its remedial measures.

Unmanageable Class-roll

Our classes become unmanageable due to large rolls. The reasons for this are manifold.

Reasons for Large Class-roll

(i) *Limited vocational choices offered:* Our students follow a routine linear path from their matric to their postgraduation. Except for the students that are absorbed in the limited professional courses (i.e., medical and engineering), the rest follow a straight path. There are very little options that they can choose from. Most of the states in India including Kashmir follow the 10+2+3 pattern recommended by the Education Commission 1964-66 as follows:

Lower Secondary 10 years (class I to X– 6 to 16+).

Senior Secondary 2 years (class I to XII – 17+ and 18+).

First Degree 3 years (19+ to 21+).

The aim of the Commission in suggesting this pattern of education was to provide three terminals in the formal school and college education with three distinct options for a student at each terminal: (1) he can step off the school system and enter working life; (2) he can step off the stream of general education and enter vocational education; and (3) he can read for a higher academic degree. The Commission felt that at the end of the ten years of school education some 40% of the students will step off the school system and enter working life, some 30% more will step off the system of general education and join vocational courses such as carpentry, smithy, typing and shorthand, etc., of one to three years' duration. Classes I to X, thus form a period of the first ten years of general education. Classes XI and XII provide for specialized studies in different subjects at the senior secondary stage. Class XII is the second terminal on this pattern with the same three distinct options available to a student. It is after class XII that some 20% of the students join professional and technical institutions, e.g., medical, engineering and technology. These students joining vocational courses after Class X or those joining technical/ professional institutions after Class XII could be given ESP as per their needs and preferences. For many, the decision is made by the family circumstances particularly the family financial position and for some by the marks secured at the undergraduate level. At this stage, questionnaires could be circulated among the students to know their preferences and ESP courses provided accordingly. An ESP course would not deal with uninspiring collection of scientific, technical and other terminology. It would be, as Singh has said, closely related to the life of the student:

> In the place of dense scientific or technical subject-matter, requiring specialist scientific or technical knowledge, the ESP that may be built around general ecological/ environmental subject matter which may be possibly of interest to the teachers and the students. The exercises may provide such problems which the students could solve themselves by using English.[1]

The Education Commission 1964-66 had envisaged that 10% of the students would seek higher education but in practice as the Hindustan Times reported "the number of the students seeking an undergraduate degree is very large for lack of vocationalization of courses at the lower secondary stage and for other various socio-economic reasons."[2]

The students who cannot get into the professional colleges enter the mainstream and flood our college rolls. A large number of them are not well-motivated and not well-defined as far as their goals are concerned. They have just two options to choose from:

(i) They may read for a graduate and postgraduate degree in the arts, science or commerce or Bachelor of Law, Business Management, etc., or

(ii) Look for a job since an undergraduate degree is a minimum qualification for all sorts of jobs in the public as well as the private sector.

The first remedial measure to reduce class-roll would therefore, be to provide various technical and vocational courses. This would be provided after Class X and would help to direct students who want vocational training for various socio-economic reasons.[3] These technical courses would include short-term vocational courses as shown below:

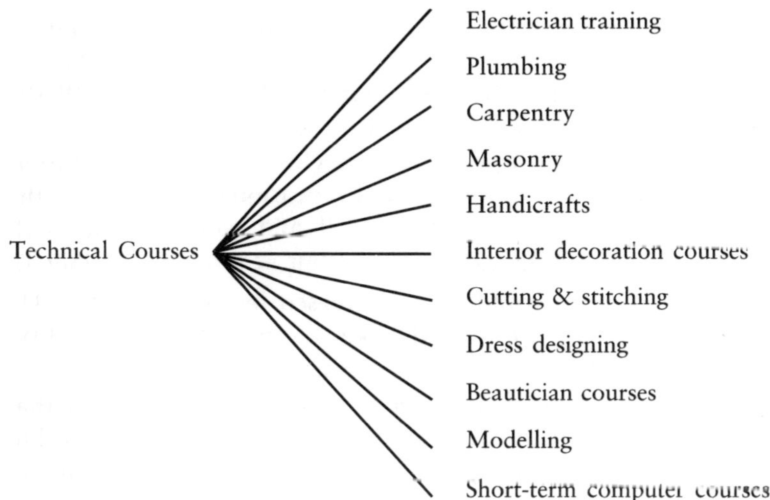

These short-term vocational courses would help a great deal in engaging those students who want quick monetary returns and also those who are not desirous of higher education.

A second remedial measure for reducing class-roll would be charging fee for Higher Secondary Education. This would act as a filter. Only those students who are actually keen to study would pursue studies. The bulk of the students (who flood our colleges because they have nothing better to do) would be made to take different courses, i.e. go for technical courses. Scholarships would be provided to poor but meritorious students who are keen to study but lack the financial resources to do so. This fee would be a minimum of Rs 300 per month for higher studies and Rs. 150 for technical courses. The fee for technical courses would be half that of higher studies so that all students who are not well-motivated for studies would be drawn towards the technical courses. The fees, thus collected would be used for upgrading the institutions in terms of lab equipments and other audio-visual aids.

At the intermediate level, a "Bridge Course for Technical Education" would be provided in addition to other courses. Students not interested in further studies shall go for the Bridge Courses after their Class XI. These students would be joining the students who had left the mainstream of education at the 10+ stage in favour of the technical courses, once they would complete the Bridge Courses. Both the groups of students (those who had opted for vocational courses at 10+ stage and those who opt for it after class XI) would be given another course of technical and vocational training. This would be called Technical Course II and would include the same courses as Technical Courses I but at a higher plane.

Our class roll would have decreased by now. In order to further reduce it, we would take a screening test[4] before entrance to colleges. This is very essential. The screening test would test the general proficiency of the students and would not be a very difficult one. Simple but basic issues would be tested. This would reduce the class roll to a very large extent.

These remedial measures, if strictly followed, would reduce the problem of large unmanageable classes.

The second problem which acts as an implementation constraint for the communicative methodology is the heterogeneity which characterizes our learner groups.[5] Our students are varied as regards their proficiency. The students coming from private schools are better exposed to the language (getting 10 years of exposure) than those students coming from government schools (getting later 2 years of exposure). In colleges they are all grouped together. This has an adverse effect on both of them. Since this problem has its roots in the school, therefore, changes need to be made at the grassroots level. These would include:

1. Introducing English as a subject from nursery class in all schools.
2. Making English as a medium of instruction in all schools.
3. Framing a uniform syllabus for all schools (Govt. & Private).
4. Appointing all teachers (both of private & Govt. schools) through a selection board.
5. Keeping M.A. as the basic qualification for appointment as teachers in all schools.

6. Giving the same salaries to private teachers as to Govt. school teachers.

The aim is to efface any discrepancy between private and Govt. schools. The same standards need to be applied in all aspects of material selection, syllabuses, teachers and evaluation. This can help in solving the problems of heterogeneity at the college level.

The Kothari Commission[6] has also made some suggestions in this regard. It has recommended the teaching of separate courses in English for different branches of education, suiting the needs of our students. The purpose of this teaching would be to train students in their specific fields. English for specific purposes would require a variety of courses for students with different backgrounds—those coming from the so-called English medium schools and those coming from Government schools. As the two categories have different degrees of proficiency in the language, the teaching programme should be devised in such a way that each category gets training in it which is adequate to its needs. Such courses would require not only streamlined teaching methods but also special units that are fully equipped to teach such courses so that the aims and objectives of its teaching are achieved in as short a period of time as possible.

I do not, however, agree with the Kothari Commission's suggestion. The registration of students coming from private schools and those coming from Government schools is neither feasible nor desirable. It will create inferiority complex in those coming from Government schools and a sense of pride in those coming from private schools.

A practical solution to the problem of heterogeneity has been put forth by the CDC report.[7] It suggests a placement test to be taken by all students entering colleges. According to their performance in the placement test they would be graded into three proficiency levels or system, namely Stream I, Stream II and Stream III. Five courses will be provided in the colleges namely:

A. Review Unit
B. Communication Skills Unit—level I
C. Communication Skills Unit—level II
D. Advanced Unit
E. Functional Unit

Students will join these courses according to their proficiency level or streams allotted to them. Thus Stream I (the lowest stream) will start with Unit A for first year and reach Unit B the next year. Stream II will start on Unit B the first year and reach Unit C the next year. Stream III will start on Unit C the first year and reach Advanced Unit the next year. Thus, there will be different entry and exit points for the three streams. While the weak students will have to put five years of college study, the more proficient will put four years while the most proficient will put only three years.

Our next problem is our undefined curriculum. At present we have an explicitly undefined curriculum.[8] Our curriculum will have to be clear and well-defined. It will have to state the aims and objectives of our teaching. A learner-centred curriculum reflecting a communicative methodology will have the following goals in view:

1. It will provide meaningful communication, texts will be authentic, tasks communicative and outcomes negotiated and not predetermined.
2. The content will be subject-based across the curriculum.
3. The first language will be used as an aid when necessary for understanding the target language particularly at the early stage.
4. A modular format will be used which will consist of a skill cycle and a thematic unit. The skills and the themes will be well integrated.
5. Learners will be made the focal point. Respect for the individual will be highly valued. Learner needs will be considered.
6. Learning will be viewed as a self-realization experience in which the learner has considerable say in the decision-making process.

7. Other learners to act as a support group within which they interact, help and evaluate themselves and each other as well as the whole person.
8. Intermediate steps to be provided to imbue participants in a communicatively oriented course—to change the attitudes and expectations of learners; build on new role definitions for learners and teachers as well (by building roles into the instructional material).
9. Awareness courses will be integrated with the general courses to educate learners for their new roles.
10. Responses will be taken from the learners during and at the end of the course to provide feedback which will be incorporated into the learning process.
11. The teacher will act as a facilitator who is more concerned with classroom atmosphere than with the adherence to the syllabus or the materials in use.
12. An attitude of co-operation and sharing between learners and teachers will be aimed at.
13. Teachers will be trained to create a conducive and anxiety-free atmosphere in the class.
14. Teachers will be provided pre-service and in-service training in language teaching courses.
15. Emphasis will be on 'doing' more than on 'knowing' or 'caring.'
16. Teachers will be provided with props supports and realia to make their proceedings work smoothly.
17. Holistic approach to learning will be aimed at.
18. Self-evaluation and peer-evaluation will be sought.
19. Language learning theory to incorporate a mentalistic-cognitive view which is compatible with a holistic approach to learning in general. Emphasis will be shifted from linguistic...competence to socio-cultural appropriateness and communicative competence.
20. The curriculum will, therefore, be based on the socio-cultural views of the nature of language;

cognitive-based views on the nature of language learning and humanistic views of education.

"The New Curriculum" framed by the UGC under the guidelines of the CDC addresses almost all these goals. Excepting the goals mentioned in points 2, 4, 8, 9, 10 and 17, all the objectives have been labelled in the New Curriculum. These points which I feel have been missed out shall be discussed in this chapter with a hope that they will be considered for implementation.

The new curriculum does not provide any measures or awareness courses to imbue participants in a communicatively oriented course. The new curriculum with its changed outlook can take the students unawares and the results can be frustrating. To avoid such a situation I recommend the introduction of "awareness courses" running parallel to the language courses and being incorporated in the timetable. In these awareness courses time will be devoted to raising learners' awareness of ways of identifying resources and strategies needed to achieve these goals and to assess their own progress. Learners will be aware of the different learning strategies, namely direct strategies and indirect strategies. The direct strategies will relate to the ways in which the learner deals with and works on the target language itself and indirect strategies will relate to the general management of learning. Within the category of direct strategies there are memory strategies which help learners to store and retrieve new information; cognitive strategies which learners use to understand and to produce new language and compensation strategies which are used when learners counter (face) gaps in their knowledge of the target language and which enables them to deal with this deficiency. The indirect strategies include metacognitive strategies which relate to the organisation of the learning process in strategic terms; affective strategies by which learners regulate their emotions, motivations and attitudes and "social strategies" which direct learners interaction with other people for the purposes of language learning. Different strategies that they (students) will need for the different skills of listening, reading, speaking and writing will be provided to them.

Besides, awareness programmes will make students aware of how to evaluate their own performance. Self-evaluation sheets will be distributed among the students; proficiency in different skills will be evaluated by the following self-assessment sheets:

Examples of Self-assessment Form (Listening Comprehension)

Instructions: Put a cross in the boxes corresponding to your estimated level in each of the four skills (listening, speaking, reading, writing).

Statement	Box	Level
I understand practically everything that is said to me in English.	☐	10
	☐	9
	☐	8
	☐	7
	☐	6
I understand spoken English fairly well.	☐	5
	☐	4
	☐	3
	☐	2
	☐	1
I do not understand spoken English at all.	☐	0

A set of four forms of this kind, one for each of the four language skills will be used to assess the learners' command of the language. However, instead of assessing the global concepts like "listening comprehension" we could use "understanding an English lesson," "reading an English daily paper" or even "retelling a story"—anything that suits the classroom context.

Example of Self-assessment Form (Speaking Skill)

Speaking

Imagine that you meet an English-speaking person who doesn't know anything about Kashmir. He wants to have as much information as possible about Kashmir and therefore, asks you questions about living conditions, housing, nature, weather, eating habits, leisure, holidays, sports, radio, television, etc. To what degree would you be able to answer his questions?

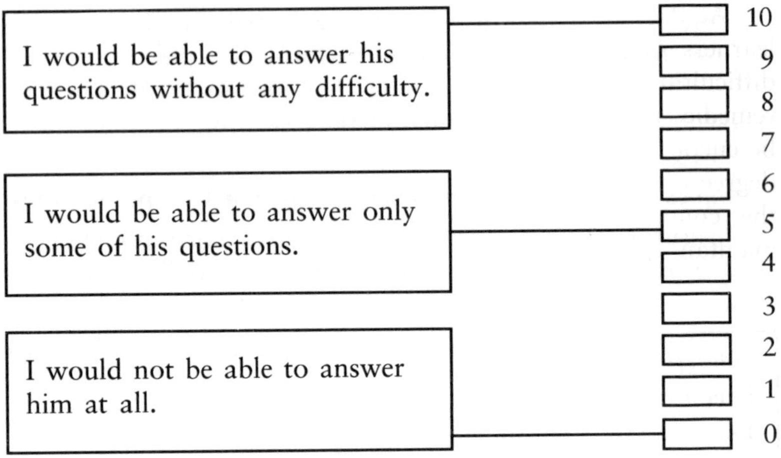

Statement	Scale
I would be able to answer his questions without any difficulty.	10
	9
	8
	7
	6
I would be able to answer only some of his questions.	5
	4
	3
	2
	1
I would not be able to answer him at all.	0

Instead of choosing between the dichotomy of 'yes,' 'no' and 'fairly well' we could use a scale with several options like 'yes,' 'probably,' 'not sure,' 'uncertain,' 'no,' 'probably not,' etc.

Apart from self-assessment at the beginning of a course there will be ongoing assessment at the end of each class. Each student will respond to the following format.

Directions

Give rating from:

1. Not at all
2. Marginally
3. Rather well
4. Perfectly well

(1) I understood what was wanted at all times. 1 2 3 4

(2) Every student was involved at some point. 1 2 3 4

(3) I was interested in the lesson. 1 2 3 4

(4) I engaged in pair-work/group-work. 1 2 3 4

(5) I talked a lot and this gave me confidence in myself. 1 2 3 4

This kind of assessment sheet will give us an idea as to the techniques employed by the teacher.

At the end of each week, each learner will have to fill his learners diary. This will help to provide feedback and the difficulties faced by the majority will be taken note of and remedies incorporated into the next week's plan. Learners will be encouraged to assess their achievements and to monitor the degree to which they can manage to use the target language in the community. The following format[9] will be used and maintained in the learner's diary:

Learner's Diary

<table>
<tr><td colspan="4">This week, I studied ___________.
This week, I learned _____________.
This week, I used English in these places ___________.
This week, I spoke in English with these people ________.
This week, I made these mistakes ________________.
This week, I gained/not-gained confidence in conversing with people ________________.</td></tr>
<tr><td colspan="4">My difficulties with English this week.</td></tr>
<tr><td>Where?</td><td>With whom?</td><td>What for?</td><td>What was the problem?</td></tr>
<tr><td></td><td></td><td></td><td></td></tr>
</table>

Such evaluation will assist in the development of a critical self-consciousness by learners acting as active agents within the learning process.

Though the "New Curriculum" has explicitly stated that it will promote greater learner-involvement and that the courses will be learner-oriented it has not given a detailed account of how this will be done. I would therefore, like to elaborate on this point more openly.

Since the learner plays a pivotal role in a learner-centred curriculum, his attitudes, aptitudes and his capabilities need to be listed. Information related to learner's needs, attitudes, educational and economic background is important and will have to be collected at the beginning of the course. A questionnaire will be circulated to each student and responses collected. This questionnaire will include questions like:

Name: ________________

Age: ________________

Sex: ________________

Nationality: ________________

Your interests: ________________

Your attitude to English or English-speaking world: ________

Your learning background: ________________________

How much time do you devote to learning English? ________

How many opportunities do you get for speaking English outside your classroom? ________________

What methodology will appeal to you? (Discuss with your teacher in your learning awareness class.) ________________

What sorts of techniques are likely to bore/alienate you? (Discuss with your teacher.) ________________

The teacher will need to maintain a record of each student separately. This questionnaire can act as an important feedback for the teacher to note the deficiencies already existing in her/his students and then work on to remove these loopholes. The detailed knowledge of the students will give the teacher a good idea of how to provide a programme of balanced activities that will be most motivating and most beneficial for her students.

Before a teacher actually starts with her work, she will need to make a plan. She will need to think about what she is going to do. Based on her knowledge of the students and the syllabus, she will consider four major areas; activities that she will include; language skill that will be developed; language that will be used and the subject and content she had for teaching the skills. When she has considered these areas she will decide whether such ideas are feasible given the institution and its restrictions. When this has been done, she possesses her pre-plan. She can now move on to the plan as shown in the figure on the next page.[10]

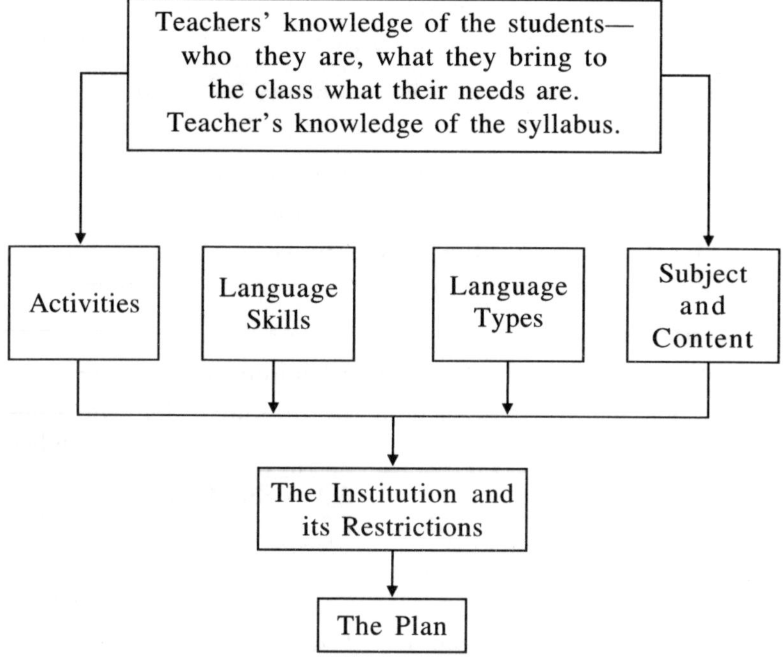

The teacher is now clear as to what she is going to do in her class. She is ready to make a detailed lesson plan. Since no provision has been made in the new curriculum regarding this, I feel it necessary to frame a lesson plan since every teacher should go to the class with a lesson plan. A typical lesson plan will include:

A. Description of the Class

Students:	Between ages 18 and 19.
Duration:	1 hour daily, seven days a week. (The duration will be changed from 40 minutes to 1 hour for the language class.)
Attitude of students:	Enthusiastic but often tired; concentration suffers sometimes.

B. Recent Work Done by Them

Introduction of 'there is'/'there are' using maps, short paragraph writing describing places.

Invitation language used.

Practice of 'simple present tense.'

A listening exercise in which students follow directions.

C. Objectives

1. Teaching socio-cultural appropriateness. (10 minutes)
2. Teaching correct situational use. (10 minutes)
3. Teaching in different situations. (20 minutes)
4. Teaching grammar. (20 minutes)

D. Contents

Objective 1. (Estimated time 10 minutes)

Match these situations with the responses that you think would be most appropriate:

Situation	A Possible Response
1. Asking the cost of a washing machine from the shopkeeper.	Excuse me please.
2. Asking the time from a stranger.	I am sorry. Hope you haven't been hurt much.
3. Apologising for spilling milk.	Excuse me. Could you please tell me the time?
4. Finding the way out in a crowd.	Excuse me. What is the cost of this washing machine?
5. Wanting to help a passenger, who is standing in a bus with his many bags.	I am sorry.
6. Seeing a colleague after the death of her mother.	Excuse me please.
7. Apologising to the boss for being late.	Could I help you with your bags?
8. Wanting to leave a party.	I am sorry to hear about the death of your mother.
9. Hurting someone accidentally.	I am sorry Sir, but there was a traffic jam on the way.

Look at the above situations and mark the different ways in which 'excuse me' is being used.

Objective 2. (Estimated time 10 minutes)

Teach correct situation use. Work in pairs and decide what to say in the following situations:

1. You come running down the stairs and bump into someone. You apologize by saying:

   (a) It's your fault. (b) I am sorry. (c) Thank you.

2. You are offered biscuits to eat. You would like burgers instead. What would you say?

   (a) How silly! (b) I am sorry. (c) No, thank you.

3. You cannot hear your boss on the phone. What would you say?

   (a) Can't you speak louder?

   (b) I can't hear you.

   (c) I beg your pardon, Sir, could you be a bit louder please?

4. Your friend has brought you a gift. You don't like it though. What would you say?

   (a) It's not good.

   (b) Sorry, I don't like it.

   (c) Thank you for it, anyway.

5. You want to leave the class while the class is on. What would you say to your teacher?

   (a) May I go out?

   (b) Please leave me for a while.

   (c) May I please be excused, ma'am!

6. Someone offers you help but you don't want it. You would say?

   (a) I don't need it.

   (b) Please leave me alone.

   (c) Thanks for the offer but I would rather do this myself.

Objective 3: (Estimated time 20 minutes)

Making use of formal, semi-formal and informal language for different occasions and relations given below:

1. One of the students keeps disturbing you in the class with the result you cannot concentrate on what the teacher says. You feel you must complain to the teacher and also tell your friend about it.
   1. What would you say to the teacher after class?

      ____

      ____

   2. What would you say to your friend after class?

      ____

      ____

2. You find that your teacher is helping one of the students in the examination hall. You want to take up the issue to the principal. You also want your parents to know.
   1. What would you say to the principal after you leave the examination hall?

      ____

      ____

   2. What would you say to your parents?

      ____

      ____

3. You have read an excellent article written by a student you know and by a professor you don't know. You want to compliment them both.

   What would you say to the student?

   ____

   ____

   What would you say to the professor?

   ____

   ____

Follow-up

Look again at the above three situations and determine how you would respond in your own language. Are there formal and informal ways of expressing yourself? Which situations call for formal speech and which call for informal speech?

Objective 4. Teaching Grammar (Estimated time 2 minutes) Read the passage below:

The Earth Our Home

Every part of this earth is sacred to my people. Every shining fine needle, every sandy shore, every mist in the dark woods, every clearing and every humming insect is holy in the memory and experience of my people. Your dead forget the country of their birth when they go to walk among the stars. Our dead never forget this beautiful earth, for it is the mother of our people. We are part of the earth and it is part of us. The perfumed flowers are our sisters; the deer, the horse, the great eagle, these are our brothers; the rocky crests, the juices in the

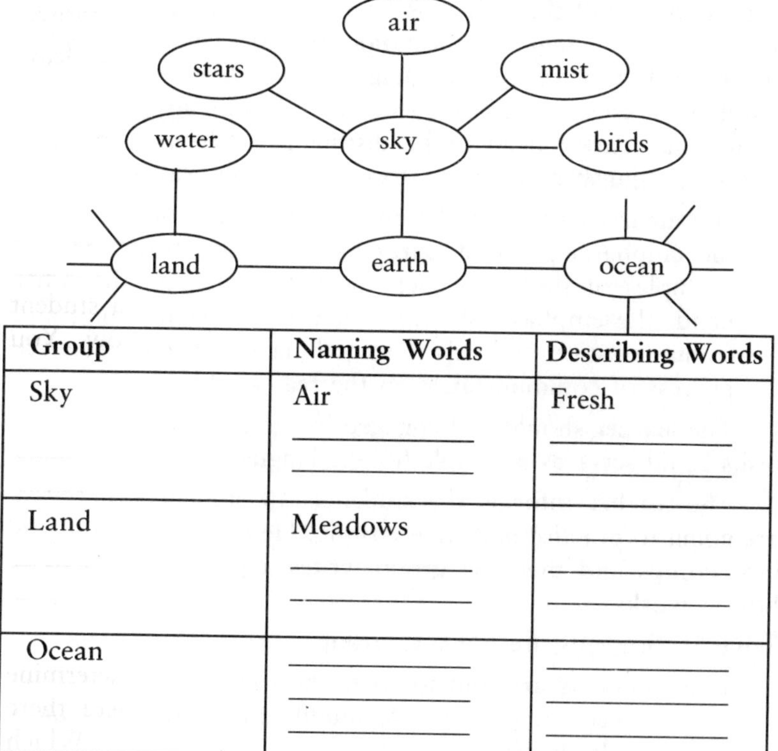

Group	Naming Words	Describing Words
Sky	Air ______ ______	Fresh ______ ______
Land	Meadows ______ ______	______ ______ ______
Ocean	______ ______ ______	______ ______ ______

meadows, the body heat of the pony and man—all belong to the same family.

Given above is a word web based on words from the passage you just read. The first word in the web is earth. It is connected to three words land, sky, and water. The words which line up with sky, are filled in. Find words which line up with land and ocean. Then fill in all these words into the naming words column in the chart shown. For each naming word, find an associated descriptive word from the passage or your own word knowledge.

An English class will have to be full of language activities and tasks. Learners will be engaged in acquiring the various language skills. Each lesson will include principles of authenticity, task continuity, real word focus, language focus, learning focus, language practice and problem solving. The English class will thus, be task-based. Since the leaner will be involved in exchanging information and ideas he/she will feel an integral part of the language union. This will help in instilling a sense of confidence and effacing any feeling of alienation. 'Tasks' need to be distinguished from 'activities.' Willis distinguishes 'activities' from 'tasks.' She says:

> Grammar exercises, drills and practice activities in which the emphasis is on a particular linguistic form, are all examples of the latter (activities). In tasks, on the other hand, the emphasis should primarily be on meaning and communication and this is something which replicates the process of communication in the real world.[11]

The learner should feel engaged in the task. The following tasks could serve as a sample for the language class.

The teacher informs the students (40 students) that they are going to practise narrative writing. He divides the students into groups and then the group writes a joint story. This is how it works:

Stage 1: Students are put into groups.

Stage 2: Students are told to write the following sentence on a piece of paper: "He found himself deserted on a lonely desert."

Stage 3: Students are then told to continue the story by writing the next sentence.

Stage 4: Students are told to give the piece of paper to the students in the right. Each student adds a line to the story.

Stage 5: The teacher tells the last in the group to write a concluding line.

Stage 6: The story is now returned to the originator by being circulated to their left.

Each group produces a different story which is read to the other groups. This task can be immensely enjoyable since wildly different stories will be formed. Apart from the element of enjoyment, it will develop in the students the skills of writing, reading, listening and speaking. The whole class will be actively engaged and participating.

A similar kind of task can be performed in which students write reports. Students are told to write items for a news broadcast which they then organise for "transmission."

Stage 1: The teacher asks all the students in the class to write two news items on a piece of paper.

Stage 2: The teacher then collects all the pieces of paper and forms the class into five groups.

Stage 3: The teacher then distributes the pieces of paper equally between the groups in no special order. The students are asked to combine the news items (making changes where necessary) to make up a complete news broadcast.

Stage 4: Each group reads its broadcast to the rest of the class.

Stage 5: One member from each group joins to make a new group to form a whole news bulletin.

Stage 6: This could be actually recorded and presented to the class to make it more realistic.

Besides being interesting, it develops the skill of expository writing, reading, listening and speaking. All the skills are thus integrated in the tasks.

Thus the communicative language class would follow an integrated lesson plan. Each language lesson will:

- derive input from authentic sources;
- involve learners in problem-solving tasks in which they are required to negotiate meaning;
- incorporate tasks which relate to learners' real-life communicative needs;
- allow learners to rehearse in class, real-world language tasks;
- require learners and teachers to adopt a range of roles and use language in a variety of settings in and out of the classroom;
- expose learners to the language as system;
- integrate the four macroskills;
- involve learners in creative language use.

Though the lesson plan has not been framed in "The New Curriculum" the curriculum is exhaustive and comprehensive. Clark's seven broad communicative activity types[12] which he proposes for language programmes, are all taken care of by "The New Curriculum." These include:

- solving problems through social interaction with others;
- establish and maintain relationships and discuss topics of interest (section 2.2.4 of Communicative Skills Unit Level I & Level II);
- search for specific information for some given purpose;
- listen to or read information, process it and use it in some way (2.2.4 of "Communication Skills Unit Level II");
- give information in spoken or written form on the basis of personal experience, (e.g. write a report or fill in a form, i.e. 2.2.2 of "Advanced Unit");
- listen to, read or view a story poem, etc. (2.2.3 of "Advanced Unit");
- create an imaginative text 12, (i.e. in 2.2.3 of "Communication Skills Unit Level I").

Pattison[13] proposes seven activity types, namely questions and answers; dialogues and role-plays; matching activities; communication strategies; pictures and picture stories; puzzles and problems; discussions and decisions. These are all taken care of by "The New Curriculum."

The course content is also detailed. It is skill-oriented rather than literature–oriented. Though skills have been greatly emphasized, literature has also been given its place in the "Reading for Enjoyment" section of both the "Communication Skills Unit Level I and Level II." The skills have been further specific in detail under the 'sub-skills.' The 'Review Unit' is an excellent remedial course for weak students to bring them on a par with the bright ones. I, however, disagree with the "Functional Unit." It should not have been placed in the Final Year of the General English course. It should have been optional and open to students of all levels with at least the competence needed for "Communication Skills Unit Level II." This would help in engaging those students who don't want to study further but who would like to take up a vocation. This would also help in reducing the class-roll at levels II, III and at the 'Advanced Unit' level.

The division of the courses between General English and Special English is very apt. "General English" is compulsory for all students at the undergraduate level while Special English is optional and will be taken up by those students desirous of further studies in the English language and its literature. The "Special English" though language and literature based provides for communication as well in the "communication" component just as the "General English" has a provision for literature. "So the Special English has a provision for language as well as aspect of communication."

I, however, disagree with framing of Unit III of "Special English." It should also have been framed along the same pattern with increase in the steepness of contents. The "Functional Courses" that the UGC recommends at this stage would be incorporated in the "Functional English Course" (already mentioned).

I also feel that the course design lacks in providing explicit and clear directions for teacher in the shape of a teacher's book. This is very essential as it directs the teacher as to how to go about her work. Without proper guidance, the implementation of the new curriculum will be a failure. For this reason, I would like to incorporate a list of teacher guides in the course design. These will include course book for teachers and trainer's books. These would provide the teachers with a number of different options on teaching and the teacher would choose the one best suited to her peculiar situation. Besides, I would suggest Adrain Doff's[14] *Teach English: A Training Course for Teachers*. Penny U's[15] *A Course in Language Teaching: Practice and Theory* and Martin Hewing's[16] *Pronunciation Tasks: A Course for Pre-Intermediate Learners.*

I also find the "Testing" section of the new course design lacking in certain ways. Since the "New Curriculum" claims to be learner-oriented and learner-centred, evaluation and testing should not have been restricted to the learner alone. Evaluation and assessment will have to be carried on at various planes. All aspects of curriculum will have to be evaluated—the teachers need to be evaluated, the materials, the method, and classroom techniques, all need evaluation.

Since teachers are the backbone of any educational system, their evaluation is of crucial significance. Though they face a selection board before being appointed yet I feel, that is not sufficient, there should be continuous ongoing assessment of all teachers including the heads of department by supervisors who should be appointed especially for this purpose. There should be at least one supervisor for each college. The assessment of teachers will be implemented in various ways:

1. Teacher's action plan.
2. Teacher filled questionnaires.
3. Observation by peers or supervisor(optional).
4. Teacher's assessment by student questionnaires.
5. Supervisor's report.

6. Principal's signatures providing a valid APR (Annual Performance Report) for the teacher.

Teachers will have to provide their action plan in which they will map out their aims, objectives and planned actions in relation to the overall goals.This action plan will take stock of their duties, interests, short-term objectives and long-term goals. Besides, teachers will be directed to maintain a professional development folder containing evidence of professional activity. These will include sample supplementary materials used in the class, lesson plans of the teacher and the teacher's contributions to any journals for any other professional activity. This folder will reveal a teacher's level of professionalism and will act as a useful professional record for each teacher.

Besides, teachers will fill in a questionnaire which will help in maintaining their academic records. The questionnaire will include questions like:

Name

(1) What is your learning background? (Give details right from school to university.) ____________

(2) What are your professional qualifications? (Begin with M.A.) ____________

(3) Are you in know of the various methods of English language teaching the world over? ____________

(4) Are you in know of the various latest techniques used in the classroom the world over? ____________

(5) What techniques do you use presently? ____________

(6) What is your attitude to the subject content? ____________

(7) What materials will you be using and what aids do you have at your disposal? ____________

(8) What innovations, if any can you contribute? ____________

These questionnaires will be filled by the teacher and collected at the beginning of each year. Teachers' annual progress will be assessed by comparing the new questionnaires with the previous ones and developments recorded. Teachers with static remarks will be taken note of and suitable action will be taken, if their staticity continues. All these will be done by the supervisors. A detailed record of each will be kept by the supervisor. This could be even fed into the computer with the supervisor's remarks for each teacher and would be kept confidential.

Besides the teacher's own record, she will be observed by the supervisor only if the head of the instutition deems it desirable. The supervisor will then rate the observation and reflect accurately what went on. The following statements would be included in the checklist:

Key

1 Does not reflect what went on.
2 Marginally reflects.
3 Reflects rather well.
4 Reflects perfectly well.

1.	There were no cultural misunderstandings.	1 2 3 4
2.	The class understood what was wanted at all times.	1 2 3 4
3.	All instructions were clear.	1 2 3 4
4.	Every student was involved at some point.	1 2 3 4
5.	All students were interested in the lesson.	1 2 3 4
6.	The teacher carried out comprehension checks.	1 2 3 4
7.	Materials and learning activities were appropriate.	1 2 3 4
8.	Student groupings and sub-groupings were appropriate.	1 2 3 4
9.	Class atmosphere was positive.	1 2 3 4
10.	The pacing of the lesson was appropriate.	1 2 3 4
11.	There was enough variety in the lesson.	1 2 3 4
12.	The teacher did not talk too much.	1 2 3 4
13.	Error correction and feedback was appropriate.	1 2 3 4
14.	There was genuine communication.	1 2 3 4

15. There was teacher skill in organising group work. 1 2 3 4
16. There was opportunity for controlled practice. 1 2 3 4
17. Students were enthusiastic. 1 2 3 4
18. General classroom management was good. 1 2 3 4

The teachers will also be assessed by their students. This is very crucial, since the students know their teachers better than anyone else as far as their efficiency is concerned. The students will fill a questionnaire given to them by the supervisor in the middle of the session. The following questions will have to be answered:

1. Name of the teacher: ____________________
2. What kind of rapport does she maintain with you during the session?
   (i) Cordial and friendly
   (ii) Cold and indifferent
   (iii) Neutral
3. Was she authoritative and thrusting?
   Yes, ______ No, ______
4. Was she learner-oriented allowing enough room for learner's participation?
   Yes, _____; Not much, ______; Not at all, ______
5. Does she correct your errors at once?
   Yes, _____; Not always, _____; Not at all, ______;
6. Does she engage in genuine communication in class?
   Yes, ___; Not always, ___; Most of the time, ___
7. Is there enough variety in her lesson?
   Yes, ______; Not much, ______; Not at all, ______
8. Are you interested and enthusiastic about her lessons?
   Yes, ____; Not much, ______; Not at all, ______;
9. Does she arrange you in groups or pairs?
   Yes, ______; Seldom, _____; Never, ______;

10. How would you rate your teacher?

    Innovative, ____; Average, ____; Not satisfactory, ___

Considering all the above assessment sheets for all the teachers the supervisor will frame his/her report for each and every teacher. He/she may be helped by the head of the institution in doing this. His/her report will be based on the teacher's own statements, as well as by the students' evaluation of their teaching. All this will help the supervisor grade the teacher. This grade will enter into the service record of the teacher at the end of each academic year and the principal's signatures will attach it a validity to be considered as the APR (Annual Performance Report) for the teacher. The grading could range from:

A+ Outstanding
A Satisfactory
B Not very satisfactory
C Poor performance

A teacher getting B or C continuously for 3 successive years will be deemed disqualified for his/her job. The once-and-for all appointment of a teacher will, therefore, be dispensed with. Teachers will be kept active in upgrading themselves and the fear of being disqualified will undoubtedly improve their performance.

Not only will the teachers be evaluated but also the materials. This evaluation will be done by the teachers as well as students.

Evaluation by teachers/students:

1. Name of the class for which the material is prescribed.
2. Is the price of the materials appropriate for your students /for you? Yes, _______; No, _______
3. Are the integral parts of the materials (course books, tapes, teacher's book, etc.) available in the market? Yes, _______; No, _______
4. Do the materials provide a balance of activities that is appropriate for your students/for you? Yes, _______; No, _______

5. Is there a sufficient amount of communication output in the materials under consideration? (i.e., does the material provide enough scope for speaking and writing) Yes, ______; No, ______
6. Does the materials provide enough roughly-tuned input for your student? Yes, ______; No, ______
7. Where the materials encourage practice, is the practice motivating for your students? Yes, ______; No, ______
8. Do the materials include the skills your students need? Yes, ______; No, ______
9. Is the language used in the materials at the right level for your students? Yes, ______; No, ______
10. Is the subject and content of the materials interesting for your students? Yes, ______; No, ______
11. Do the materials contain clear guidance for the teacher about how they can use them (materials) to their best advantage (e.g. in a teacher's book)?
12. Would you recommend continuing with these materials? Yes, ______; No, ______

The response of the teachers and the students will provide the necessary feedback for continuing or discontinuing with these materials. Valid and necessary changes will be incorporated into the course design.

Since the teacher is the most important factor in the implementation of any curriculum, it becomes imperative that any changes made in the curriculum be acceptable to the persons who have to practically carry it out. Teachers should therefore, be informed of any changes likely to take place and their consent taken before finalising the changes, otherwise the results will be frustrating. In other words, the teachers should be actively involved in the framing of the curriculum, after all, it is the teachers who have to bear the burden of it all. If innovations are made, teachers should be properly trained to adapt themselves to these changes. The CDC Report comments aptly in this regard:

> For a successful implementation of the curriculum proposed in this Report, it is imperative that the teacher be properly trained. The new curriculum not only has some new objectives, new course content and a changed focus but it also suggests some new teaching material, methods of teaching and devices for testing. The significance of that which is new in the proposed curriculum must in the first place be fully appreciated by the teacher herself before she can implement it. Indeed in some cases the teacher may have to familiarize herself with the new subject matter before she can teach it. To put it more emphatically the new curriculum fails if the teacher is not trained to implement it. Hence, the need for teacher training.[17]

The Report categorises four teacher groups for whom training has to be provided.

(i) A majority of the existing teachers who have not formally studied the structure of the English language and the teaching and learning of it.

(ii) Teachers of the future who will have undergone the proposed M.A. courses and will, therefore, have studied the structure of Modern English as a compulsory paper, but will not have studied English Language Teaching (ELT) since it is an elective paper

(iii) Teachers of the future who will have studied ELT as well as the structure of Modern English as part of their M.A. programme.

(iv) Teachers holding qualifications such as PGDTE CIEFL.[18] (Post Graduate Diploma In Teaching English)

Dhamija in her thesis mentions that most of the teachers "continue in the profession on the strength of academic degrees acquired much before they joined the profession. Only 4% of the teachers have attended any orientation programmes or workshops on ELT. This goes to show the paucity of teacher training programmes leading to the lack of interest in changes in language teaching methodology and pedagogy. The range of teaching experience is from 2 years to 32 years but the winds of change in ELT are not reflected anywhere at all."[19]

Of the four categories of teachers mentioned in the CDC Report, we in India generally have teachers belonging to the first category. They are actually without any ELT qualification, the best training programme for them is the PGDTE course offered by the CIEFL. The teachers could be relieved of their college duties in the slack session every year. The teachers could be given intensive full-time five months of training so that by the start of the new session they would be fully equipped to implement "The New Curriculum."

The truth is that unless the traditional teacher-centred teaching is abandoned in favour of a learner-centred approach, no effective change in the existing situation can be brought about. Creating of ELT cells in our universities would be the first step towards ELT planning. Such cells would be necessary both for teaching and research work in ELT if we have to reconcile theoretical principles with local constraints and conditions.[20] We must identify our local constraints and see how best and how far they should be reconciled, a job no outsider can do for us. Moreover, teacher training has to be a continuous process.

I would suggest this teacher training to start just after the selection of a teacher by the Public Service Commission. I would call this the pre-service training. This pre-service training would start immediately after a teacher's selection and would last for one full year. This would make the teacher's teaching career meaningful and purposeful from the very first day of his teaching career. This pre-service training would be carried on along the lines suggested by Hunt.[21] Teacher trainees would be exposed to models of teaching and would be treated as EFL students. This approach would be cyclic, that is, say, on the first day a listening speaking lesson would be given, on the second day a reading writing lesson, on the third day a lesson designed to help with learner autonomy and so on. Thus the time-table would be repeated but not the individual lessons. Thus trainees will be exposed to models of an overall lesson (e.g. a listening lesson) and important basic classroom techniques (related to the skill in question) will be demonstrated.

For example, in a vocabulary lesson modelled by the trainer, the trainees will learn how to:

- be well-organized and prepared with a lesson plan;
- use a picture to generate lots of vocabulary;
- expose students to a word many times in many ways in order to reinforce meaning;
- limit the use of new vocabulary in a lesson;
- structure a lesson;
- involve students in all possible ways.

This 'modelling lesson' as it were, will have to be followed in teaching practice sessions in which the trainees will practise teaching on the same lines as the trainer. Various difficulties that the trainees are likely to face will get highlighted and remedies sought jointly by the trainer and the trainees. These pre-service training courses will inculcate certain basic techniques and skills that a teacher needs essentially to focus on.[22] Once these basic skills are mastered we can now focus on 'teacher development.'

Aslam distinguishes teacher training from 'teacher development.' 'Teacher development' is a more comprehensive process in which teachers from different parts of the country pool their experience (i.e., interact) in order to become aware of each others situation.[23] It becomes a process of sharing, interacting and negotiating ones experience with fellow teachers in order to grow independently and autonomously. For this Aslam rightly suggests (and I personally agree with Dr. Aslam in this regard) the framing of working groups at the state level, the regional level, and the national level. 'The State Working Group' would include all the English teachers (the college teachers) who would meet annually to share their syllabuses, methods, materials and techniques with each other. At this stage, experts in educational philosophy would be asked to contribute by way of discussion, their expert comments for the overall betterment of the teaching programme. The available literature on ELT would be made available through hand-outs, books or photo copies of journal articles.

'The Regional Group' would comprise teachers from four different regions—North, South, East and Western Central. Each region would be represented by ten or more teachers selected from the state level group. The groups would discuss the findings of the state level groups. All aspects of teaching English in India would be discussed. This would include the curriculum, syllabuses, materials, textbooks, methods, classroom, techniques, and testing. Since there would be varied viewpoints, a lot of discussion and debate would ensue and a consensus would be sought. Again, experts from within and outside India would be invited to comment on the findings of these groups.

'The National Level Group' would be framed out of the regional groups–say, five teachers from each region. This group would discuss the findings of the earlier groups and come out with their recommendations/suggestions about the ELT in India. On the basis of the findings of the State and the Regional Groups, the National Group would recommend a uniform (a) ELT curriculum to be adopted; (b) the syllabus; (c) the textbooks and other material to be used; (d) the method to be adopted. About the techniques the teacher should be given some freedom to follow her own techniques but at the same time keeping the aims and objectives always in view.

In this way, a uniform ELT curriculum would be adopted with clear aims and objectives and success or failure of the proposed curriculum would be discussed at all the three levels. The national level group would decide each year whether or not the previous curriculum would be followed.[24] Any changes needed thereof would be implemented. In this way, the curriculum development would be a continuous process with the feedback coming from all the states in the country.

Prasad's view also deserves attention in this regard. He suggests, "the University Grants Commission or the Ministry of Education should organise a conference of all the Vice-Chancellors, Directors of Education and other educational administration closely connected with this matter in order to evolve a common and uniform pattern as far as possible."[25]

In this way, all aspects of the teaching/learning process have to be looked into. "The New Curriculum" has to a large extent, attended to the important issues and the loopholes that I personally felt were existing, have been dealt with by me after extensive thought and research. It has been felt that all aspects of the curriculum (and the curriculum itself) need to be scrutinized and evaluated. This evaluation needs to be a continuous ongoing process with regular feedback continuously incorporated into the system and necessary changes made. All this is possible provided proper co-ordination is maintained with the other states and with the centre. It needs to start with teacher education and training and gradually move on to the learners. Once teachers are properly grounded in "The New Curriculum," the ripples will be felt throughout the system. It is to these ripples that I would be looking forward in my voyage as a communicative teacher of English.

REFERENCES

1. R.K. Singh. "English for Specific Purposes: An Indian Perspective." *Fachsprache* 5, 3: 137-40.
2. *The Hindustan Times*. March 13,1984. New Delhi, 9.
3. These reasons have been discussed in Chapter 3.
4. A similar test was introduced in the University of Kashmir a few years back and the unnecessary flux of students got checked.
5. This has been discussed in detail in Chapter 3.
6. Kothari Commission Report. 1966. New Delhi: Publication Division.
7. CDC Report.1989, 58.
8. This point has already been discussed in detail in Chapter 3.
9. From Ian Tudor. 93.
10. Quoted in Harmer. 227.
11. Quoted in William Guariento and John Morley. "Text and Task Authenticity in the EFL Classroom." *ELT Journal* 55, 4 Oct 2001. Oxford University Press.
12. John L.Clark. *Curriculum Renewal in School Foreign Language Learning*. 1987.
13. P. Pattison. *Developing Communication Skills*. Cambridge University Press. 1987.
14. Adrain Doff's. *Teach English: A Training Course for Teachers*. Cambridge University Press. 1988.

15. Penny Ur. *A Course in Language Teaching: Practice and Theory*. Cambridge: Cambridge University Press, 1996.
16. Martin Hewings. *Pronunciation Tasks: A Course for Pre-Intermediate Learners*. Cambridge Univesity Press, 1993.
17. CDC Report. 1986, 327.
18. CDC Report. 328.
19. Deepti Dhamija. "The Teaching of English Literature and Communicative Language Teaching in the Indian Classroom." *Unpublished Thesis*, 1993, 135.
20. We have one centre of ELT at the Department of English in the Kashmir University but it is defunct. Teacher training programs are taken care of by Academic Staff Colleges everywhere now.
21. Quoted in Nicky Hockley. "Modelling and Cognitive Apprenticeship in Teacher Education." *ELT Journal* 54, 2 (April 2000). Oxford University Press.
22. These courses could be managed by the same centres as those used for in-service training. Only care has to be taken that the trainers are masters in their fields.
23. Mohammad Aslam. 1997, 194.
24. Thus in a learner-centred approach all the aspects of teaching/ learning including the curriculum would be subject to scrutiny and evaluation.
25. N.K. Prasad. *The Language Issue in India*. Leela Devi Publications: Delhi, 1979, 53.

Conclusion

The foregoing discussion of the various trends in English Language Teaching and the implications of adopting a communicative method reveal that a lot needs to be done to change the existing system of teaching and learning English at the college level in India. The basic issue to be considered is that the outlook of learners as well as teachers need to undergo a radical transformation. Whereas the teachers realize the need to abandon their authoritative attitude, the learners are to be motivated to accept the new responsibilities with full awareness of what the method entails. The new student-teacher relationship has to be made acceptable to both sides. This needs a lot of effort from both the sides.

Besides, one glaring fact which stands out and weighs all other considerations is the training of teachers. Since teachers are the main agents of change, no innovation can be possible without it being realised and accepted by the teachers. A very practical way of training teachers is by sending them to the CIEFL Hyderabad or to its Northern Wing at Lucknow for an intensive full-time training in the slack session each year. This could be managed on a rotation basis with half the faculty members receiving training and the other half managing the college engagements. The position would be reversed the following year. This would ensure that by the start of the new session our teachers would be fully acquainted with what and how to teach.

Teachers need to be consulted at every step and actually involved in the framing and implementation of the new method. The responses of the teachers to the questionnaire given to them reveal that they are desirous of a change in the various aspects of the curriculum. They however regret (as the interviews held with them reveal) that their seniors show a cold attitude to any change. The senior faculty members who are on the verge of retirement do not want a change in the syllabus or course books for their own reasons and unfortunately they are the people framing the syllabuses at the boards of studies. This trend has to be done away with and members to the boards of studies need to be taken on account of their professional excellence and performance. Only such members who are really experts in their fields have a right to decide what materials to include and what changes to incorporate. Seniority alone should not be the criterion for this responsibility. This again is something which is within the limits of the possible and awaits implementation. Moreover, the whole educational system needs to work in co-ordination at all levels. The school, the intermediate, the college and the university education levels have all to be well-knit and properly graded. Any shortcomings at any level will show in magnified dimensions if not treated immediately. Besides, all the colleges need to be co-ordinated both within and outside different state. The curriculum needs to be uniform throughout (and a copy of it to be in the possession of each teacher) and the same methods need to be used for its implementation countrywide. The teachers need to be qualified in ELT before attempting to take language classes. For this, special attention needs to be given at the university level to train students in this direction. The new M.A. course programme recommended by the UGC will hopefully solve half the problem.

The questionnaires distributed to the learners reveal that they need English by and large to communicate their ideas in everyday situations and express themselves clearly and effectively. For this General English Course which is skill-oriented has been framed and needs to be implemented. Students need to be properly channelized according to their proficiency levels. The syllabuses and the course materials are not to be thrust down their throats (as is presently done). They need to be given the right types of courses to suit their differing levels. This will be encouraging for both the 'weak' and 'strong' students. While the proficient learners will put in 3 years of college study, the weak ones will have to put in 5 years. This is again a very practical solution and needs to be implemented at the earliest.

The existing teaching materials have to be changed altogether. Instead of literature-based courses we have to shift to skill-oriented courses as envisaged in "The New Curriculum." Students will be actually engaged in performing the various skills. The skills and the sub-skills are already labelled in detail in "The New Curriculum" and need to be put into practice.

The mode of teaching—the method used and the techniques employed to implement the new method will have to be made acceptable to the teachers and learners. The lecture mode of teaching will have to give way to pair-work and group-work with emphasis on learner's participation.

The evaluation has to be broad-based and ongoing. A little effort from the teachers in knowing the responses of the students regarding the method used, the material used, the techniques used, etc. will provide the necessary feedback into the system. This will further indicate what changes need to be made.

To sum up, all the aspects of the curriculum have been thoroughly dealt with. Positive recommendations have been put forth. The new method outweighs the old in every aspect. What remains to be done is the assessment of these recommendations on practical grounds and once found valid, their immediate implementation. It is this aspect that we will be looking forward to in the very near future.

APPENDICES

Appendix A

Questionnaire for Teachers

1. Do you think the syllabus for General English for the Three Year Degree Classes is interesting, motivating and relevant to the needs of the students?

   Yes ☐ No ☐

   Comment. ______________________________

   ____

2. Does the syllabus teach all the four skills of language (SRWL)?

   Yes ☐ No ☐

   Comment. ______________________________

   ____

3. Does the syllabus contain clear guidance for the teacher about how the material can be used to the best advantage of the student? (for example, in a teacher's book)

   Yes ☐ No ☐

   Comment. ______________________________

   ____

4. Are the integral parts of the material available? (i.e., the course books, teacher book, tapes, etc.)

   Yes ☐ No ☐

   Comment. ______________________________

   ____

5. Does the syllabus provide a balance of activities that is appropriate for your students? (i.e., listening activities and problem-solving activities)

   Yes ☐ No ☐

Comment. ______________________________
____

6. Is there a sufficient amount of communication output in the material in the course? (i.e., does the material put the students into communication?)

   Yes ☐ No ☐

   Comment. ______________________________
   ____

7. Do the materials provide enough roughly-tuned input for your students?

   Yes ☐ No ☐

   Comment. ______________________________
   ____

8. Is the language introduced in realistic contexts? (i.e., in contexts taken from real-life situations)

   Yes ☐ No ☐

   Comment. ______________________________
   ____

9. Would you recommend continuing with these materials for your students?

   Yes ☐ No ☐

   Comment. ______________________________
   ____

10. Besides lecture method what other methods do you use in teaching English?

    ____________________ ____________________
    ____________________ ____________________

11. Would you label yourself as:

    1. Innovative. 2. Average/Routine. 3. Resourceful.

12. If you feel your students are not understanding you, do you:

    (1) At once switch over to explaining and translating the difficult words into the second language (Urdu) or the mother tongue (Kashmiri)?

    (2) Continue explaining in English giving synonyms

and like examples and avoiding translating into L2 or L1?

13. What sort of activities would you like to engage your class in? Arrange the following in order of your preference:
    (a) Copying written material, memorising, drill and repetition work.
    (b) Grammar exercises.
    (c) Communication tests and problem solving.
    (e) Language games, role play, reading topical articles and close (gap-filling) exercises.
    (f) Listening and note taking.
    (g) Reading books and newspapers.
    (h) Using audio visuals, T.V., Video, etc.

14. What sort of activities do you actually engage your class in?

    ______________________ ______________________

    ______________________ ______________________

15. What according to your view do the students respond more eagerly to? Arrange the following in order of their preference:
    (a) Copying notes, memorising, drill and repetition work.
    (b) Grammar exercises.
    (c) Listening.
    (d) Answering questions.
    (e) Discussing exercises and viewpoints among themselves.
    (f) Discussing issues and viewpoints among themselves.
    (g) Communicating their ideas with each other and discussing with the teacher.
    (h) Confining themselves to the syllabus and the examination pattern and avoiding any out of syllabus discussions.

16. Do you think our students fail to express their ideas in the English language?

    Yes ☐ No ☐

Comment. ______________________________

____

17. What in your view is the reason for this failure to communicate?

____

____

____

18. Has your method/material used helped the students to improve in any way?

Yes ☐ No ☐

Comment. ______________________________

____

19. What are the major problems faced by you as a teacher of English language? Arrange the following in order of significance:

(i) Inefficient learning strategies.
(ii) Faulty methods of teaching.
(iii) Inappropriate learning activities.
(iv) Irregular attendance.
(v) Inappropriate objections.
(vi) Poor attention in class.
(vii) Poor motivated students.
(viii) Learner attitude not positive.
(ix) Very large and unmanageable class roll.

20. Would your response to errors be

(i) Tolerant or
(ii) Corrective at all costs.

21. What do you think are the remedial measures for these problems?

(i) ______________________________
(ii) ______________________________
(iii) ______________________________
(iv) ______________________________
(v) ______________________________
(vi) ______________________________
(vii) ______________________________

(viii) ______________________

(ix) ______________________

22. Do you feel that the teacher is restricted by the syllabus and by the limitations of time as far as using his own technique in teaching the four skills is concerned?

Yes ☐ No ☐

Comment. ______________________

____

23. Indicate by giving a rating from I to 4 (I most important), who in your opinion should be primarily responsible for carrying out the following curriculum tasks. Give a rating from I to 4 for each task.

A. Teacher-in-charge of the Centre.
B. Classroom teacher.
C. Outside curriculum specialist.
D. Curriculum advisor.

Tasks	A	B	C	D
1. Initial needs analysis.				
2. Goal and objective setting.				
3. Selecting/grading context.				
4. Ongoing needs analysis.				
5. Grouping learners.				
6. Devising learning activities.				
7. Instructing learners.				
8. Monitoring/assessing progress.				
9. Course evaluation.				

24. Would you recommend continuing with the present method of teaching?

Yes ☐ No ☐

Comment. ______________________

____

25. Do you think English should be taught through literature or through language courses? Give reasons.

____

____

____

26. How do you like teaching in class? Put a circle around your answer.
    (1) Individually.
    (2) In small groups.
    (3) In one large group.
27. Would you like teaching through:
    (1) Television/Video/Films? Yes/No
    (2) Radio? Yes/No
    (3) Tapes/Cassettes (e.g., language labs, language masters) Cassette players? Yes/No
    (4) Written material? Yes/No
    (5) The blackboard? Yes/No
    (6) Pictures/Posters? Yes/No

Appendix B
Response from Teachers

1. Do you think the syllabus for General English for the Three Year Degree Classes is interesting, motivating and relevant to the need of the students?

   Yes ☐ No ☐

   Comment. ____________________

Response:	Yes	No	Comment	Didn't comment
	30%	70%	90%	10%

   It is obvious that a majority of the teachers are not satisfied with the syllabus. The 90% that commented felt that the syllabus is very lengthy. It is neither interesting and motivating nor relevant to their needs.

2. Does the syllabus teach all the four skills of language (SRWL).

   Yes ☐ No ☐

   Comment. ____________________

Response:	Yes	No	Comment	Didn't comment
	30%	70%	83.5%	16.5%

   It is obvious that the majority is of the view that the syllabus does not teach all the four skills. 83.5% of the teachers who commented, remarked that the listening skill is only marginally developed. The teachers feel that if listening would have been followed by comprehensive question-answering then it would have developed this skill to a great extent, since listening would have been with a purpose. Since listening is not followed by any comprehension question-answering, it is not sure whether the students have been actually listening or just watching.

The speaking skill is not touched at all, since there is no time for it. The teacher is hard-pressed for time, so that the speaking skill cannot be stressed.

3. Does the syllabus contain clear guidance for the teacher about how the material can be used to the best advantage of the student? (for example, in a teacher's book)

Yes ☐ No ☐

Comment. ____________________

Response:	Yes	No	Comment	Didn't comment
	10%	90%	74%	26%

It is obvious that the 10% of teachers who said 'Yes' did not quite comprehend the question otherwise they would have answered in the negative, as we know there is no such thing as a teacher's book for the guidance of the teachers. The syllabus doesn't contain any guidance for the teachers. It is wholly examination-oriented. This in turn affects the classroom teaching.

4. Are the integral parts of the material available? (i.e., the course books, teachers book, tapes, etc.)

Yes ☐ No ☐

Comment. ____________________

Response:	Yes	No	Comment	Didn't comment
	0%	100%	84%	16%

The 84% of teachers who have commented state that only the course books are available. There is no such thing as teacher's book or tapes, etc. available.

5. Does the syllabus provide a balance of activities that is appropriate for your students? (i.e., listening activities and problem-solving activities)

Yes ☐ No ☐

Comment. ____________________

Response:	Yes	No	Comment	Didn't comment
	6.6%	93.4%	66.7%	33.3%

Again I feel that the 6.6% of teachers who have answered in the affirmative have not comprehended the question well. There are no activities provided in the syllabus. The syllabus is content-oriented and not skill or activity-oriented.

6. Is there sufficient amount of communication output in the material in the course? (i.e., does the material put the students into communication?)

Yes ☐ No ☐

Comment. ______________________

Response:	Yes	No	Comment	Didn't comment
	23.3%	76%	70%	30%

I personally feel that there is nothing in the material that could lead the students into communication with each other. The 70% that commented feel that the teacher could have introduced it by his/her innovativeness and resourcefulness but because of the limitations of time and the unmanageable class roll he/she is practically helpless.

7. Does the material provide enough 'roughly-tuned input' for your students?

Yes ☐ No ☐

Comment. ______________________

Response:	Yes	No	Comment	Didn't comment
	26.6%	73.4%	90%	10%

This question posed a little problem. Most of the teachers did not understand the term 'roughly-tuned input'. I had, therefore, to explain this term and what the question asked to get their response.

It was remarked that the materials used, i.e. the textbooks, are greatly above their level of comprehension, so the teacher has to make extensive use of translation to make it comprehensible to the students. The material should have been properly graded to suit their standards so that translation would be avoided and the students would get exposed to the right kind of input.

8. Is the language introduced in realistic contexts? (i.e., in context taken from real-life situations)

Yes ☐ No ☐

Comment. ____________________

Response:	Yes	No	Comment	Didn't comment
	6.6%	93.4%	66.7%	33.3%

In fact the 6.6% of the teachers who answered in the affirmative have misunderstood the question, since the language is not presented in real life-like contexts but in dull, boring and uninteresting texts.

9. Would you recommend continuing with these materials for your students?

Yes ☐ No ☐

Comment. ____________________

Response:	Yes	No	Comment	Didn't comment
	13.3%	86.7%	93.4%	6.6%

As is obvious, the majority of the teachers are not satisfied with the materials. As most have commented that the material is far beyond their level of comprehension, so instead of a language class it becomes a translation class where the maximum time is spent in translating the difficult words into Urdu or into Kashmiri. The very essence of the language class is therefore lost.

10. Besides lecture mode, what other mode do you use in teaching English?

Response: 100% of teachers use the lecture mode. Out of these, 40% engage the class in small discussions. All feel that they are limited by the constraints of time, lengthy syllabus and huge class roll.

11. Would you label yourself as (1) Innovative (2) Average (3) Resourceful?

Response: 76.6% feel they are average.

13.5% feel they are resourceful.

10.1% feel they are innovative but they cannot use their innovativeness and resourcefulness because of the limitations of time, very short periods, unmanageable class roll and lengthy syllabus.

12. If you feel your students are not understanding you, do you:
    (1) At once switch over to explaining and translating the difficult words into the second language (Urdu) or the mother tongue (Kashmiri)?
    (2) Continue explaining in English giving synonyms and like examples and avoiding translation into L2 or L1

    Response: 60% use translation as a technique.
    33.3% use the Direct Method.
    6.7% use translation as a last resort.

    The 60% who use translation as a technique feel that they use it against their will and would like to do otherwise but because the texts are far beyond the comprehension of the students, they (the teachers) have to resort to translation to make the texts comprehensible to the students. They feel that the Direct Method becomes irrelevant in our situation. Again the 6.7% avoid using translation initially but use it as a last resort to make the students comprehend the texts. The above response shows that we make use of translation as a technique and not as a mode in teaching grammar rules. It also shows that we use an eclectic method in language teaching.

13. What sort of activities would you like to engage your class in? Arrange the following in order of your preference:
    (a) Copying written material, memorizing drill and repetition work.
    (b) Grammar exercise.
    (c) Communication tests and problem-solving.
    (d) Language games, role play, reading articles and close (gap-filling) exercises.
    (e) Listening and note taking.
    (f) Reading books and newspapers.
    (g) Using audio visuals, T.V., Video, etc.

    Response: 93.3% feel that communication test and problem-solving should be first in priority.

63.3% feel that language games, role play, reading articles and close (gap-filling exercises) should come second.

76.6% feel that grammar should occupy the third place.

63.3% feel that reading books and newspapers should come at the fourth place.

50% feel that listening should come fifth in priority while the other 50% feel it should come sixth.

50% feel that audio-visual should be sixth in priority. Out of the other 50%, 30% feel it should be second in priority.

As is clear from the responses, the majority of the teachers are wanting a switch over to the communicative methodology. They are giving clear preference to communicative activities and to grammar.

14. What sort of activities do you actually engage your class in?

Responses: When personally contacted to know what sort of activities they engaged their class in, the teachers frankly admitted that there was no scope for any activity since the constraints of time, lengthy syllabus and unmanageable class-rolls were very high.

100% teachers engage their class in lecture-listening.

15. What according to your view do the students respond more eagerly to? Arrange the following in order of their preference:

(a) Copying notes, memorizing, drill and repetition work.
(b) Grammar exercises.
(c) Listening.
(d) Answering questions.
(e) Discussing exercises and viewpoints among themselves.

(f) Discussing issues and viewpoints among themselves.
(g) Communicating their ideas with each other and discussing with the teacher.
(h) Confining themselves to the syllabus and the examination pattern and avoiding any out of syllabus discussion.

Response: 98.4% of teachers feel that the students respond most eagerly to listening, confining to syllabus, copying notes and grammar exercises and least to discussions, answering questions and any communicative activity.

1.6% feel otherwise.

16. Do you feel our students fail to express their ideas in the English language?

Yes ☐ No ☐

Comment. ____________________

Response:	Yes	No	Comment	Didn't comment
	100%	0%	100%	0%

All the teachers invariably feel that the students fail to express themselves in English.

17. What in your view is the reason for their failure?

Response: 99% of teachers feel that the main reason for the failure to communicate is deficient schooling; late start for teaching English at the school level; lack of exposure both at school and at their home.

1% feel that in addition to the above reasons one major reason is that English has been treated as a content subject and not a language subject.

18. Has your method/material used helped the students to improve in any way?

Yes ☐ No ☐

Comment. ____________________

Response:	Yes	No	Comment	Didn't comment
	67%	33%	86.7%	13.3%

67% of teachers that claim that their method/material has helped the students to improve, frankly admit that the improvement has been to a very small extent. 33% clearly state that there has been no benefit at all.

19. What are the major problems faced by you as a teacher of English? Arrange the following in order of significance:
    (i) Faulty syllabus.
    (ii) Faulty methods of teaching.
    (iii) Inappropriate learning activities.
    (iv) Irregular attendance.
    (v) Inappropriate objectives.
    (vi) Poor attention in class.
    (vii) Poor motivated students.
    (viii) Learner attitude not positive.
    (ix) Very large and unmanageable class roll.

    Response: 100% of teachers feel that the most grave problem faced is unmanageable class roll.

    80% feel that the fault lies with the method.

    20% feel that the fault lies with the learner.

20. Would your response to errors be (i) Tolerant (ii) Corrective at all costs?

    Response: 93.3% feel their attitude to errors is corrective at all cost.

    6.7% find their attitude tolerant.

21. What do you think are the remedial measures for these problems?

    Response: 100% of teachers feel that the most important remedial measure is to reduce the class roll to forty so that individual attention is given.

    98.1% feel that the time allotted to language classes is not sufficient and that it should be extended to 1 hour.

    99% feel that the problems faced in the colleges have their roots in faulty teaching of the English language at the school level. Therefore, they suggest that the remedial measures should start at the grassroots levels. English should be made compulsory from the nursery level in all schools.

90% feel that there should be a screening test for the students before entrance into colleges. The dropouts should attend a bridge course to get more competent.

89.7% feel that the syllabus is too lengthy and it results in a rush through due to lack of time. They, therefore, suggest that the syllabus be considerably reduced.

97.8% feel that the materials used are beyond the comprehension of the students, so that much time is spent in translating the difficult words into L2 or L1. They, therefore, recommend material which is appropriate to the level of the students.

96.8% feel that orientation and refresher courses be made compulsory for all teachers after every 8 months.

22. Do you feel that the teacher is restricted by the syllabus and by the limitations of time as far as using his/her own techniques in teaching the four skills is concerned?

Yes ☐ No ☐

Comment. ____________________

Response:	Yes	No	Comment	Didn't comment
	100%	0%	56.7%	43.3%

All the teachers agree on the point that they are definitely restricted by the constraints of limited time, lengthy syllabus and also unmanageable class roll. The comments reveal that in order for language teaching to be productive and effective, these three limitations have to be rectified at the earliest. No matter what methodology we use, these limitations pose a serious problem and should be dealt with as a first step towards improvement.

23. Indicate by giving a rating from 1 to 4 (1 most important) who in your opinion should be primarily responsible for

carrying out the following curriculum tasks. Give a rating from 1 to 4 for each task. .

A. Teacher-in-charge of the centre.

B. Classroom teacher.

C. Outside curriculum specialist.

D. Curriculum advisor.

Tasks	A	B	C	D
1. Initial needs analysis.				
2. Goal and objective setting.				
3. Selecting/grading content.				
4. Ongoing needs analysis.				
5. Grouping learners.				
6. Devising learning activities.				
7. Instructing learners.				
8. Monitoring/Assessing progress.				
9. Course evaluation.				

Response: 100% of teachers feel that it is the teacher who should do the initial needs analysis.

90% feel that the teacher, the curriculum specialist and the curriculum advisor should set the goals and objectives and select the contents.

84.3% feel that the teacher, the curriculum specialist and the teacher-in-charge of the institution should do the ongoing needs analysis.

85.6% feel that the grouping of the students should be done by the teacher and the head of the institute.

87.9% feel that the devising of learning activities, assessing of progress and course evaluation should be done by the teacher, the curriculum specialist and the curriculum advisor.

As seen in the above responses the role of the teacher is considered as of paramount importance. The teacher needs to be consulted at every stage of curriculum planning (curriculum spoken of in its broader sense). The majority of the problems that we presently face are mainly because we overlook the crucial role of the teacher. Presently, the teacher is merely the interpreter (or rather translator) of the text of the framing of which she has no access. She has to present what is handed down to her without having any say in it. The little innovativeness which she would like to introduce is snatched away by the various constraints under which she has to operate. This brings poor results. The role of the teacher, therefore, needs to be redefined.

24. Would you recommend continuing with the present method of teaching?

Yes ☐ No ☐

Comment. ______________________

Response:	Yes	No	Comment	Didn't comment
	24%	76%	80%	20%

Response: 76% of teachers do not want to continue with the present system because it is outdated and does not teach all the four language skills.

24% feel that in our present set-up with limited time, unmanageable class roll and lengthy syllabus, no innovation is possible, so they would continue, since there is no other alternative.

25. Do you think that English should be taught through literature or through language courses? Give reasons.

Response: 70% feel that language should be taught through language courses alone to improve the four skills.

30% feel that language should be taught through both because both are complementary and add to one another, almost all are convergent on the point that to appreciate literature, language skills should first be developed through language, courses (till the 10+2 stage). Later in the colleges, the two should be well integrated, co-ordinated and intertwined, as it were, to make it interesting and enjoyable for the student.

26. How do you like teaching in class? Put a circle around your answer.

(1) Individually (2) In small groups (3) In one large group.

Response: 89.5% prefer teaching in small groups while 10.5% feel that under the present circumstances it is not possible to form small groups (due to the constraints already discussed). So they would teach in one large group as there is again no alternative.

27. Would you like teaching from:

1. Television/Video/Films. Yes/No
2. Radio. Yes/No
3. Tapes/Cassettes (e.g. labs, cassette players). Yes/No
4. Written material. Yes/No
5. The blackboard. Yes/No
6. Pictures/Posters. Yes/No

Response: While 93.4% of teachers would like to use all the mentioned aids,

6.6% would not like to use radio as an aid, perhaps because the material on the radio is not under your control.

They would rather like to use tapes and cassettes where the input is directly under control.

From the above responses the following glaring points stand out prominently:

1. The teachers are by and large dissatisfied with the syllabus, the method, the material and the class room techniques used.
2. The teachers are desirous of having communicative activities introduced in the classroom.
3. The teachers feel handicapped in the present situation under the constraints of time, syllabus and unmanageable class roll.
4. The teachers are ready to accept a change for the better.

Having discussed the teachers' response, let us now discuss the response of the students who were given the following questionnaire. About 100 questionnaires were circulated in the already mentioned colleges. The students who were contacted belonged to various streams of Arts, Sciences and Commerce. The questionnaires were distributed to the students by various teachers and later collected and handed over to the scholar.

Appendix C
Questionnaire for Students

1. Do you think the syllabus for General English for the Three Year Degree Classes is interesting, motivating and relevant to your needs?

   Yes ☐ No ☐

   Comment. ________________________________

   ____

2. Do you feel that the syllabus teaches all the four skills of language, i.e. Speaking, Reading, Writing and Listening?

   Yes ☐ No ☐

   Comment. ________________________________

   ____

3. Are the integral parts of the materials, i.e. the course books available?

   Yes ☐ No ☐

   Comment. ________________________________

   ____

4. Does the syllabus provide a balance of activities that is appropriate for you? (i.e. listening activities and problem solving activities)

   Yes ☐ No ☐

   Comment. ________________________________

   ____

5. Are the materials designed in such a way so as to provide sufficient amount of communication output? (i.e., does the material put the students into communication?)

   Yes ☐ No ☐

   Comment. ________________________________

   ____

6. Are the materials designed for you:
   - (a) Slightly above your level of comprehension?
   - (b) Greatly above your level of comprehension?
   - (c) Just right for your level of comprehension?
   - (d) Below the level of your comprehension?
7. Is the language presented to you in realistic life-like situations? (i.e., in contexts taken from real-life situations)

   ____

   ____
8. Are you satisfied with the material recommended for you?

   ____

   ____
9. Besides lecture method, which other method does your teacher use in teaching English?

   ____

   ____
10. If you do not understand what your teacher says, does she/he:
    - (i) Switch at once, to explaining and translating the difficult words into the second language (Urdu) or the mother tongue (Kashmiri)?
    - (ii) Continue explaining in English giving synonyms and like examples and avoiding translating?
11. Would you label your teacher as:

    1. Innovative 2. Routine/Average 3. Resourcesful?
12. What sort of activities does your teacher engage you in class? Arrange the following in order of preference:
    - (i) Copying writing material, memorizing drill and repetition work.
    - (ii) Grammar exercises.
    - (iii) Listening and note taking.
    - (iv) Communication tasks and problem-solving activities.
    - (v) Language games, role-play, reading activities and gap-filling exercises.

13. What learning activities do you prefer?
    (i) Copying written material, memorizing, dull and repetition work.
    (ii) Grammar exercises.
    (iii) Reading from books.
    (iv) Listening.
    (v) Answering questions.
    (vi) Discussing issues and view points among your classmates.
    (vii) Communicating your ideas with each other and discussing with the teacher.
    (viii) Confining yourself to the syllabus and the examination pattern and avoiding any out of syllabus discussions.
14. Has the method/material your teacher used helped you to improve upon your skills?

    Yes ☐ No ☐

    Comment. ____________________

    ____
15. Is your teachers' response to your errors:

    1. Tolerant? 2. Corrective at all costs?
16. Are you satisfied with the way your teacher teaches you?

    Yes ☐ No ☐

    Comment. ____________________

    ____
17. Do you feel that you fail to express yourself in English?

    Yes ☐ No ☐

    Comment. ____________________

    ____
18. What in your opinion is the reason for this failure to communicate?

    ____

    ____

    ____

19. What are the main problems faced by you as a student of English language which have led to failure in achieving desirable results? Arrange the following in order of significance:
    (i) Insufficient learning strategies.
    (ii) Faulty methods of teaching.
    (iii) Inappropriate learning activities.
    (iv) Irregular attendance.
    (v) Inappropriate objectives.
    (vi) Poor attention in class.
    (vii) Poor motivation on your part.
    (viii) Lack of positive attitude on your part.
    (ix) Very large and unmanageable class roll.
20. How do you think these problems could be overcome and rectified?
    (i) ________________________________
    (ii) ________________________________
    (iii) ________________________________
    (iv) ________________________________
    (v) ________________________________
    (vi) ________________________________
21. What is your educational background?
    (i) Come from govt. schools.
    (ii) Come from private schools.
22. How will you rank yourself as far as your hold on English language is concerned?
    (i) Above average (ii) Average (iii) Below average
23. For what purpose do you wish to learn English?
    (i) Passing the exams.
    (ii) For other reasons, specify. ____________________
    ____
    ____
24. Where do you need to use English on long basis? Is it in your:
    (i) Medical profession?
    (ii) Engineering profession?

(iii) Software profession?
(iv) Teaching profession?
(v) Business profession?
(vi) Tourism or some other profession?
(vii) None of the above.

25. Indicate by giving a rating from 1 to 4 (1 most important), who in your opinion should be primarily responsible for carrying out the following classroom tasks?

A. Teacher-in-charge of Institution.
B. Classroom teacher.
C. Outside curriculum specialist.
D. Curriculum advisor.

Tasks	A	B	C	D
1. Initial needs analysis.				
2. Goal and objective setting.				
3. Selecting/grading content.				
4. Ongoing needs analysis.				
5. Grouping learners.				
6. Devising learning activities.				
7. Instructing learners.				
8. Monitoring/assessing progress.				
9. Course evaluation.				

26. How do you like learning in class? Put a circle around your answer.

(1) Individually (2) In pairs
(3) In small groups (4) In one large group

27. Would you mind if other students sometimes correct your written work? Yes/No

28. Would you mind if the teacher sometimes asks you to correct your own work? Yes/No

29. Would you like learning from:

(1) Television/Video/Films? Yes/No
(2) Radio? Yes/No

(3)	Tapes/Cassettes (e.g. language labs, language masters) Cassette player?	Yes/No
(4)	Written material?	Yes/No
(5)	The blackboard?	Yes/No
(6)	Pictures/Posters?	Yes/No

APPENDIX D
Response from Students

1. Do you think the syllabus for General English for the Three Years Degree Classes is interesting, motivating and relevant to your needs?

   Yes ☐ No ☐

   Comment. ______________________

Response:	Yes	No	Comment	Didn't comment
	72.5%	27.5%	77.5%	22.5%

   The students seem to be satisfied with the syllabus.

2. Do you feel the syllabus teaches all the four skills of language, i.e. Speaking, Reading, Writing and Listening?

   Yes ☐ No ☐

   Comment. ______________________

Response:	Yes	No	Comment	Didn't comment
	67.5%	32.5%	80%	20%

   Once again students feel satisfied that the syllabus teaches them all the four skills, when we know that the listening and speaking skills have been totally ignored in the syllabus.

3. Are the integral parts of the materials, i.e. the course books available?

   Yes ☐ No ☐

   Comment. ______________________

Response:	Yes	No	Comment	Didn't comment
	80%	20%	67.5%	32.5%

   The students seem satisfied with the availability of their course books.

4. Does the syllabus provide a balance of activities that is appropriate for you? (e.g., listening activities and communicative activities)

   Yes ☐ No ☐

   Comment. ______________________

   Response: Yes No Comment Didn't comment
   62.5% 37.5% 72.5% 27.5%

   A positive response has come from the majority of the students though there are no activities in the syllabus that teach the speaking and listening skills. Perhaps the question was difficult.

5. Are the materials designed in such a way so as to provide sufficient amount of communication output? (i.e., put them into communication with each other)

   Yes ☐ No ☐

   Comment. ______________________

   Response: Yes No Comment Didn't comment
   62.5% 37.5% 67.5% 32.5%

   A positive response has come from the majority of the students, though the materials provided in the syllabus do not put them into communication with each other. Perhaps the question was difficult for the students.

6. Is the material designed for you:

   (a) Slightly above your level of comprehension?
   (b) Greatly above your level of comprehension?
   (c) Just right for your level of comprehension?
   (d) Below the level of your comprehension?

   Response: 55% of students say that the material is just right for their level of comprehension.

   27.5% say that the material is slightly above their level of comprehension.

   17.5% say that the material is greatly above their level of comprehension.

The response seems to be fifty-fifty. While almost 50% feel that the material provided in the syllabus is just right for their comprehension, almost 50% feel it is above their comprehension.

7. Is the language presented to you in realistic life-like situations? (i.e., in contexts taken from real-life situations)

Yes ☐ No ☐

Comment. ____________________

Response:	Yes	No	Comment	Didn't comment
	45%	55%	32.5%	67.5%

The 45% of students who believe that the language is presented in realistic life-like situations seem to be confused with the material being realistic and it (material) being presented in a realistic life-like situation. Perhaps due to this lack of comprehension the majority of the students (67.5%) did not comment at all.

In no case is the language presented in realistic life-like situations. It is content-based but not context-based.

8. Are you satisfied with the material recommended for you?

Yes ☐ No ☐

Comment. ____________________

Response:	Yes	No	Comment	Didn't comment
	47.5%	52.5%	77.5%	22.5%

Almost 50% seem to be satisfied and 50% not satisfied.

9. Besides lecture mode which other mode does your teacher use in teaching English?

Comment. ____________________

Response: 100% of students admit that the lecture mode is the only mode used in teaching English. They, however, feel that lengthy syllabus, limited time and huge class roll is responsible for this.

10. If you do not understand what your teacher says, does he/she:

(i) Switch at once to explaining and translating the difficult words into L2 or L1?

(ii) Continue explaining in English giving synonyms and like examples and avoiding translating?

Response: While 67.9% say that the teacher at once switches to Urdu or Kashmiri. 32.1% say that the teacher uses synonyms or like words in English and avoids translation.

11. Would you label your teacher as:

(i) Innovative (ii) Routine/Average (iii) Resourceful

Response: 57.5% label their teacher as resourceful.

32.5% label them as average.

10% label them as innovative. Although the students admit that the teacher is resourceful yet he/she cannot benefit the student much due to the constraints under which he/she is working.

12. What sort of activities does your teacher engage you in class? Arrange the following in order of preference:

(i) Copying written material.

(ii) Grammar exercises.

iii) Listening and note taking.

(iv) Communication tasks and problem-solving activities.

(v) Language games, role-play, reading activities and gap filling exercises.

Response: 80% feel that the first preference is given to listening and note taking.

70% feel that the second preference is given to grammar.

63.8% feel that the third preference is given to copying written material and drill.

Options (iv) and (v) were left unmarked since these activities do not take place at all.

13. What learning activities do you prefer?

(i) Copying material, memorising and repetition work.

(ii) Grammar exercises.

(iii) Reading from books.

(iv) Listening.
(v) Answering questions.
(vi) Discussing issues and viewpoints among your classmates.
(vii) Communicating your ideas with each other and discussing with the teacher.
(viii) Confining yourself to the syllabus and the examination pattern and avoiding any out of syllabus discussions.

Response: While 87.5% would prefer communicating and discussing and engaging in communicative tasks, 12% would like to engage in listening, reading and grammar exercising.

5% would like to confine themselves to the syllabus.

This response from the students is very crucial. It shows that the students are ready to accept the communicative methods of teaching. They would prefer discussing, communicating their ideas and engaging in grammar exercises. This response shows the psychological readiness on the part of the students to accept the communicative techniques.

14. Has the method/materials your teacher used helped you to improve upon your skills?

Yes ☐ No ☐

Comment. ______________________

Response:	Yes	No	Comment	Didn't comment
	85%	15%	85%	15%

The 85% of students who feel they have been benefited have clearly commented that the benefit is limited to writing and vocabulary development. Their speaking skill is not developed.

The 15% who say that they have not been benefited again are speaking in terms of their speaking skill. They lack the ability to communicate their ideas in English and hence admit not to have been benefited.

15. Is your teachers' response to your errors:
    (1) Tolerant
    (2) Corrective at all costs?

    Response: 75% feel that their teachers' response is corrective at all costs, while 25% feel that they are tolerant of their errors.

16. Are you satisfied with the way your teacher teaches you?

    Yes ☐ No ☐

    Comment. ____________________

Response:	Yes	No	Comment	Didn't comment
	80%	20%	80%	20%

    80% feel that they are satisfied with the way their teacher teaches them. Yet they have a few suggestions to make. Some of them would like role-play to be introduced in the class while drama is being taught. Most would like some sort of communicative activity to go on in the class.

    This response is again very crucial since it shows the psychological readiness on the part of the learner to accept the communicative techniques. However, they all believe that the teacher is restricted by various limitations so that he/she cannot exploit his/her full potential. The 20% that believe they are not satisfied feel that the English class is a mere translation of difficult words into Urdu. The students are not made to speak, so the speaking skill remains undeveloped.

17. Do you feel that you fail to express yourself in English?

    Yes ☐ No ☐

    Comment. ____________________

Response:	Yes	No	Comment	Didn't comment
	52.5%	47.5%	70%	30%

    Out of 47.5% who claim that they can express themselves in English, 14% did not comment at all. 33.5% who commented could not make proper sense of what they were saying. In fact the students' responses served a good example for examining and assessing the errors of the students. Some of the comments of the students who feel they can express themselves perfectly well in English are quoted.

"It helps us to pronunciate proper English words."

"Because I properly understood the words which are too difficult, with the help of dictionary."

"I personally make efforts of talk."

"I think on English usually."

The situation is quite clear. Although 47.5% claim to be able to express their ideas in English, actually only 19% can really express themselves manageably well.

18. What in your opinion is the reason for this failure to communicate?

Response: 20% feel that this failure is due to poor schooling.

15% feel that it is due to the faulty methods of teaching.

10% feel it is due to lack of exposure both at school and home.

12.5% feel that this question does not apply to them since they can communicate their ideas perfectly well.

The comments of 5% were unintelligible.

12.5% feel it was due to lack of confidence.

25% did not comment at all.

19. What are the main problems faced by you as a student of English which have led to failure in achieving desirable results? Arrange the following in order of significance:

(i) Faulty syllabus.
(ii) Faulty methods of teaching.
(iii) Inappropriate learning activities.
(iv) Irregular attendance.
(v) Inappropriate objectives.
(vi) Poor attention in class.
(vii) Poor motivation on your part.

(viii) Lack of positive attitude on your part.

(ix) Very large and unmanageable class roll.

Response: 22.5% feel that the fault lies with the learners.

14% are not clear about the problems faced though they are sure that unmanageable class role is of paramount importance.

40% feel that the fault lies with the methods.

12.5% did not comment.

11% feel that they faced no problems at all.

20. How do you think these problems could be overcome and rectified?

Response: 35% say that the class roll should be limited to thirty so that individual attention is given.

25% say that the material should be such as will promote all the four skills. They suggest that communicative activities be promoted so that interaction takes place and their speaking skill gets improved.

10% say that the syllabus should be reduced to half so that the teacher has enough time to use his/her innovative ways.

30% of the response was unintelligible and irrelevant.

21. What is your educational background?

(i) Come from govt. schools.

(ii) Come from private schools.

Response: 52.5% come from government schools while 47.5% come from private schools.

22. How will you rank yourself as far as your hold on English language is concerned?

(i) Above average (ii) Average (iii) Below average

Response: 82.5% have labelled themselves as average.

10% have labelled themselves as above average.

7.5% have labelled themselves as below average.

I personally feel (from my experience as a teacher) that 82.5% are below average, 7.5% are average and 10% are above average.

23. For what purpose do you wish to learn English?

    (i) Passing the exams (ii) For other reasons

    Response: 12.5% study English to pass the exams.

    10% did not comment at all.

    62.5% study English so that their communicative skill gets developed and they are in a position to communicate their ideas to the rest of the world and also to gain social status.

    12.5% study English in order to be able to benefit from the scientific knowledge and the technological development that are available in the language.

    2.5% want to study English surprisingly to know about the culture of the English.

24. Where do you need to use English on long term basis. Is it in your:

    (i) Medical profession.
    (ii) Engineering profession.
    (iii) Software profession.
    (iv) Teaching profession.
    (v) Business profession.
    (vi) Tourism or some other profession.
    (vii) None of the above.

    Response: 30% of students want to use English in the teaching profession.

    20% want to use English in the business profession.

    15% want to use English in the tourism profession.

    2.5% want to use English as journalists.

    10% want to use English in the software profession.

15% don't want to use English in any of the above-mentioned professions.

7.5% of the students did not respond at all.

A majority of the students want to use English in the teaching profession. It is imperative, therefore, that they be taught through productive teaching methods so that they carry the same on to the next generation.

25. Indicate by giving a rating from 1 to 4 (1 most important), who in your opinion should be primarily responsible for carrying out the following classroom tasks:

A. Teacher-in-charge of the institution.

B. Classroom teacher.

C. Outside curriculum specialist.

D. Curriculum advisor.

Tasks	A	B	C	D
1. Initial needs analysis.				
2. Goal and objective setting.				
3. Selecting/Grading content.				
4. Ongoing needs analysis.				
5. Grouping learners.				
6. Devising learners.				
7. Instructing learners.				
8. Monitoring/Assessing progress.				
9. Course evaluation.				

Response: 52.5% did not seem to understand the question. Their response was a random single tick.

22.5% did not respond to this question at all.

15% felt that it was the teacher, the curriculum specialist and the curriculum advisor who should make important decisions like initial needs, analysis, goal setting, selecting and grading, devising learning activities and assessing and evaluation, whereas the teacher in consultation with the teacher-in-charge of the institution should do the ongoing needs analysis and grouping learners. These students feel the teacher to be of paramount importance.

10% feel that it is the curriculum specialist and the curriculum advisor that should take the decisions of goal setting and grading contents, devising learning activities and assessing progress and course evaluation while the teacher should do the initial and the ongoing needs analysis and the grouping of learners.

26. How do you like learning in class? Put a circle around your answer.
    (1) Individually.
    (2) In pairs.
    (3) In small groups.
    (4) In one large group.

Response: 67.5% want to read in small groups.

17.5% want to study in one large group.

5% want to read individually.

5% did not comment.

A majority of the students want to read in small groups. This again is a welcome sign for introducing communicative methodology. The students (majority) are psychologically ready to accept the techniques employed in the communicative methodology.

27. Would you mind if other students sometimes correct your written work? Yes/No

Response:	Yes	No
	15%	85%

The majority of the students would not mind if other students corrected their work. This again is a positive response if we want to introduce the communicative method. The students are seen to respond positively to all the crucial issues involved in communicative methodology. This once again shows that they are psychologically ready for a change although they do not themselves perceive it.

28. Would you mind if the teacher sometimes asks you to correct your own work? Yes/No

Response:	Yes	No
	12.1%	87.9%

Again the majority of the students would not mind correcting their own work. Once again the students are ready to accept the classroom techniques employed in the communicative method.

29. Would you like learning from:
    (1) Television/Video/Films? Yes/No
    (2) Radio? Yes/No
    (3) Tapes/Cassettes (e.g., language labs, cassettes players)? Yes/No
    (4) Written material? Yes/No
    (5) The blackboard? Yes/No
    (6) Pictures/Posters? Yes/No

Response: 80.3% are ready to learn from T.V.
63.1% would like to learn from the radio.
81.7% would like to learn from tapes.
87.5% would like to learn from written material.
72.5% would like to learn from the blackboard.
55% would like to learn from pictures/posters.

I feel 'pictures/posters' to have been ranked low either due to misunderstanding the word 'picture' or else they feel it would not be feasible at this late stage.

Once again the responses show that the students are ready to accept the innovative classroom techniques.

Some of the responses are shown in the ensuing charts:

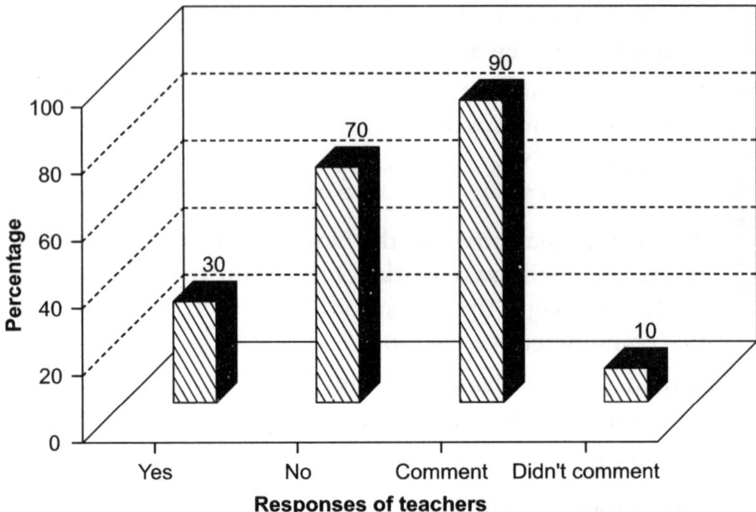

Chart showing that the syllabus for General English for the Three Year Degree Classes is neither interesting and motivating nor relevant to the needs of the students.

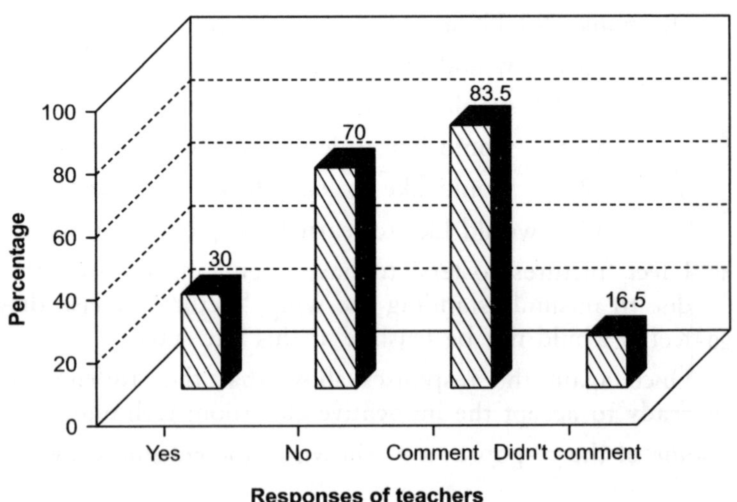

Chart showing that the present syllabuses of General English do not teach all the four skills of language.

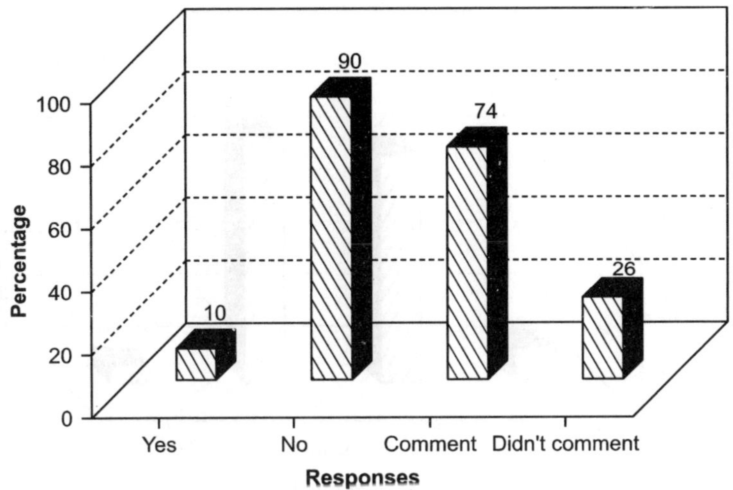

Chart showing our present syllabuses' lack of guidance for teachers.

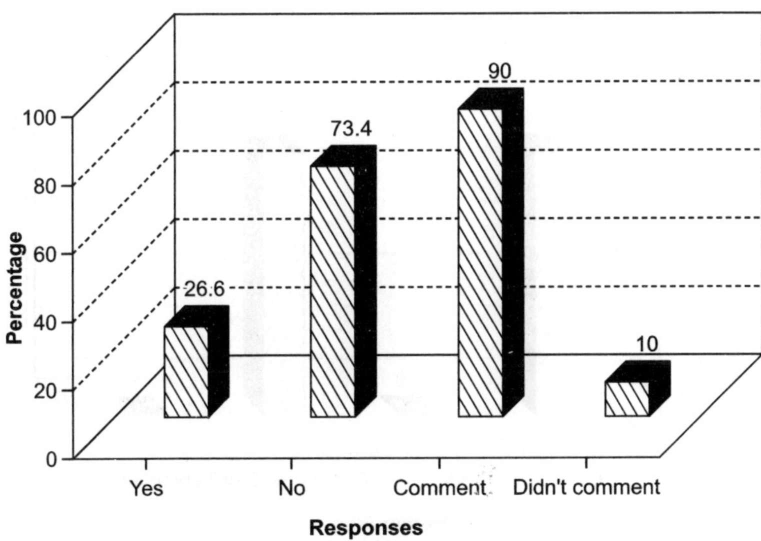

Chart showing the comprehensibility of the material to be greatly above the level of comprehension of students.

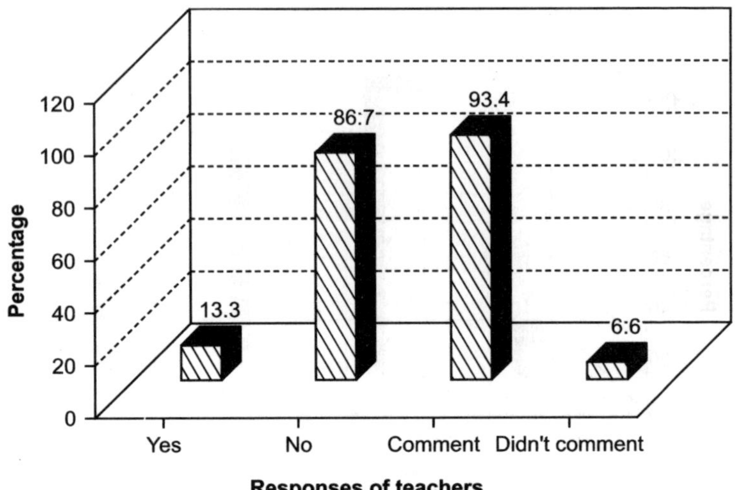

Chart showing that materials are not be continued with.

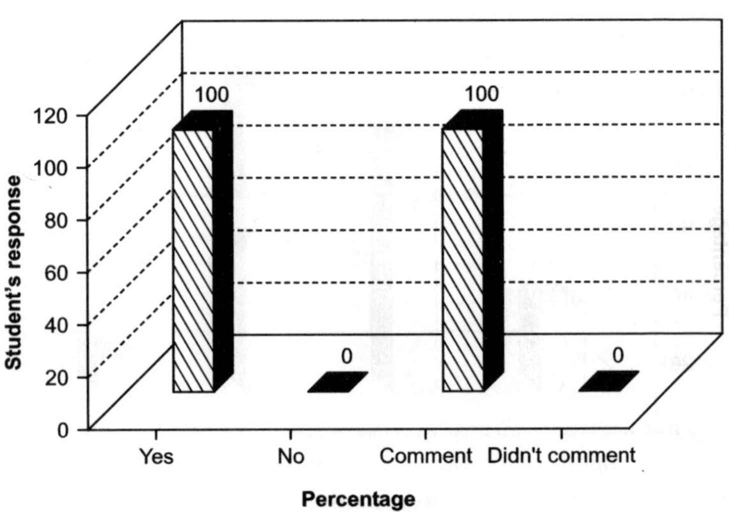

Chart showing that our students cannot communicate in English.

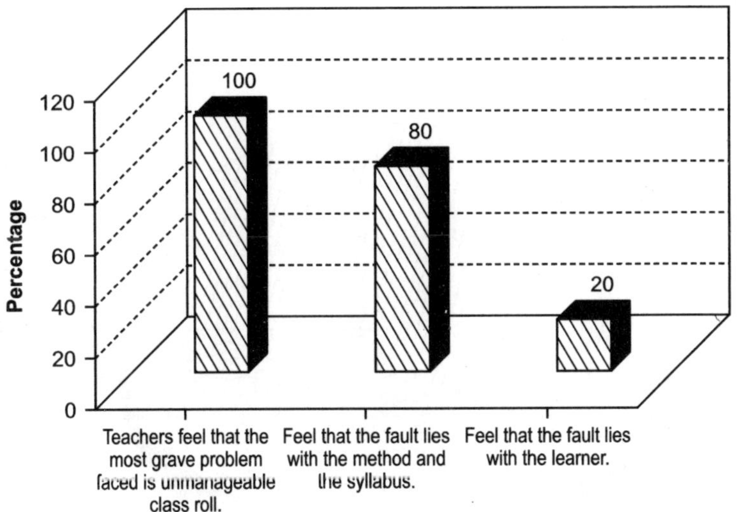

Chart showing the reasons for the failure of students to communicate.

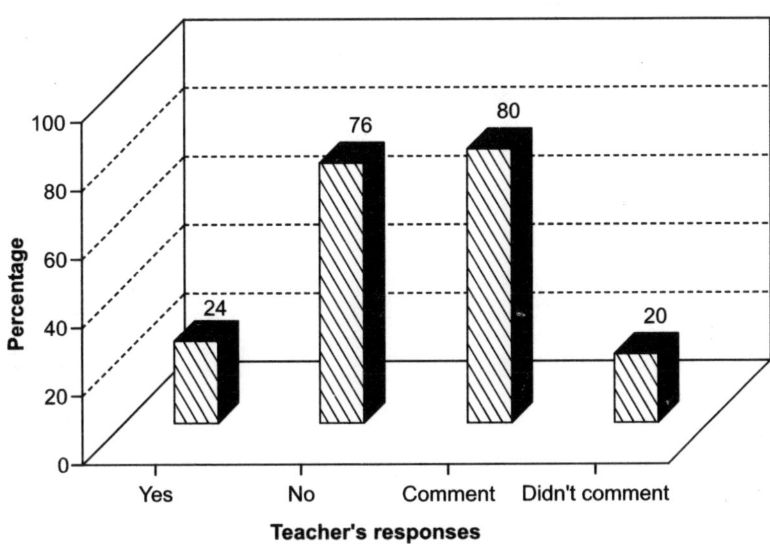

Chart showing that the present method of teaching should not be continued with.

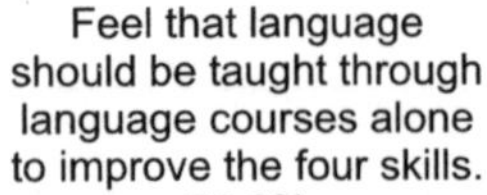

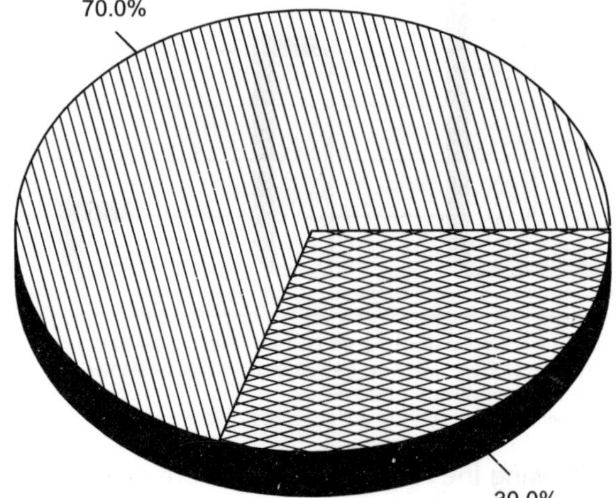

Chart showing that the language should be taught through language courses alone to improve the four skills.

Bibliography

Alatis, J.E., H.B. Altman and P.M. Alatis (eds.). *The Second Language Classroom Directions for the 1980s*. Oxford: Oxford University Press. 1981.

Allen, J.P.B. "A Three-Level Curriculum Model for Second Language Education." *Canadian Modern Language Review* 40(1): 23-43.

Allen, J.P.B. "General-Purpose Language Teaching: A Variable Focus Approach" in *ELT Documents* 118, 68.

Allen, J.P.B. "Functional-Analytic Course Design and the Variable Focus Curriculum" in *ELT Documents* 124, 10.

Allen, B. Harold (ed.). *Applied English Linguistics*. Amerind Pubiishing. 1958, 350.

Allwright, R.L. "Language Learning Through Communication Practice" in *ELT Documents* 76, 3: 2-14.

Anthony, E.M. "Approach, Method and Technique" *English Language Teaching*, 1963, 17: 63-7.

Aslam, M. *Developing a Learner-Centered ELT Curriculum in India: Trends and Issues*. Bareilly: Prakash Book Depot, 1997, 109-10.

Aslam, M. "Local Errors in the Use of English at the Undergraduate Level in Kashmir." *English Studies in India*. Nov. 1983, 101-09.

Aslam, M. *Trends in English Language Teaching in India*. Bareilly: Prakash Book Depot, 1989.

Bachman, L.F. *Fundamental Considerations in Language Testing*. Oxford: Oxford University Press, 1990, 90.

Banerji and Mohan. "General English Syllabuses: A Critical Review." *Journal of Higher Education* 10, 3:1985, 233-43.

Bell, T. Roger. *An Introduction to Applied Linguistics*. London: Batsford, 1981, 950.

Blair, R.W. (ed.) *Innovative Approach to Language Teaching*. USA: Newsbury House Publishers, 1982, 193.

Breen, M.P. "Process Syllabuses for the Language Classroom" in *ELT Documents* 118, 58.

Breen, M.P. and C.N. Candlin "Essential of a Communicative Curriculum in Language Teaching." *Applied Linguistics I*, 1980, 89-112.

Brink, A. *et al. Let us Try To Do It Better*. Adelaide South Australian Adult Migrant Education Service, 1985, 9.

Brown, G. and G. Yule. *Teaching the Spoken Language*. Cambridge: Cambridge University Press. 1983, 83.

Brindley, G. *"Needs Analysis and Objective Setting in the Adult Migrant Education Program."* Sydney: New South Wales. Adult Migrant Education Service, 1984, 31.

Brumfit, C.J. and Johnson R. (ed.). *The Communicative Approach to Language Teaching*. Oxford: Oxford University Press, 1979, 75.

Brumfit, C.J. (ed.). *Teaching Literature Overseas: Language-based Approaches*. Pergamon. 1983, 87.

Brumfit, C.J. *Communicative Methodology in Language Teaching: The Roles of Fluency and Accuracy*. Cambridge: Cambridge University Press, 1984, 778.

Candlin, C.N. "Syllabus Design as a Critical Process" in *ELT Documents* 118, 34.

Chomsky, N. *Aspects of the Theory of Syntax*. Cambridge: MIT Press, 1965.

Clark, John L. *Curriculum Renewal in School Foreign Language Learning*. Oxford: Oxford University Press. 1987, 52.

Corder, Pit. *Introducing Applied Linguistics*. Penguin. 1973, 296.

Cunningsworth, Alan: *Evaluating and Selecting EFL Teaching Materials*. London: Heinemann Educational Books. 1984, 16.

Dhamija, D. "The Teaching of English Literature and Communicative Language Teaching in the Indian Classroom." *Unpublished Thesis*, 1993, 135.

Doff, A. *Teach English: A Training Course for Teachers*. Cambridge: Cambridge University Press, 1988.

Dubin, F. and E. Obstain. *Course Design: Developing Programmes and Materials for Language Learning*. Cambridge: Cambridge University Press, 1986, 79-80.

Halliday, M.A.K., A. MacIntosh and P. Strevens. *The Linguistic Science and Language Teaching*. London: Longman, 1964.

Halliday, M.A.K. *Learning How to Mean*. Edward Arnold. London, 1975, 11-17.

Harmer, Jeremy. *The Practice of English Language Teaching*. Longman: New York, 1983, 209.

Hewings, Martin. *Pronunciation Tasks: A Course for Pre-Intermediate Learners*. Cambridge: Cambridge University Press, 1993.

Hockley, N. "Modelling Cognitive Apprenticeship in Teacher Education" in *ELT Journal* 54, 2 (April 2000) Oxford: Oxford University Press.

Holec, H. *Autonomy and Foreign Language Learning*. Strasbourg: Council of Europe, 1979, 27.

Hyltenstam & Pienemann (eds.). *Modelling and Assessing Second Language Acquisition*. Clevedon: Multilingual Matter, 1985.

Howatt, A.P.R. *A History of English Language Teaching*. Oxford: Oxford University Press, 1984, 279.

Hutchinson, T. and A. Waters. *English for Specific Purposes*. Cambridge: Cambridge University Press, 1987.

Hymes, D. "On Communicative Competence" in J.B. Pride and J. Holmes (eds.). 1972, 14.

Ingram, D.E. *Australian Second Language Proficiency Ratings*. Canberra: Commonwealth Department of Immigration. 1984, 44.

Jackobovits, L.A. and Gordon Barbara. *The Context of Foreign*

Language Teaching. Rowley, Mass: Newbury House, 1974, 44.

Jackobovitis, L.A. *Foreign Language Learning: A Psycholinguistic Analysis of Issues*. Rowley, Mass: Newbury House, 1970, xii.

Jain, R.K. *Essentials of English Teaching*. Vinod Pustak Mandir, 1985, 173.

Johnson, K. and K. Morrow (eds.). *Communication in the Classroom*. London: Longman, 83-99.

Johnson, K. *Communicative Syllabus Design and Methodology*. Oxford: Pergamon Press, 1982, 203.

Kachru, B. Braj (ed.). *The Other Tongue: English Across Cultures*. Oxford: Pergamon Press, 332.

Kennedy, C. "Innovating for a Change: Teacher Development and Innovation" in *ELT Journal* 41, 1987, 166-7.

Kennedy, C. "Evaluation of the Management of Change in ELT Projects." *Applied Linguistics* 9, 1988, 322.

Koul, Omkar N. (ed.). *English in India: Theoretical and Applied Issues*: New Delhi: Creative Publishers, 1992, 225.

Krashen, S.D. *Second Language Acquisition and Second Language Learning*. Oxford: Pergamon, 1981.

Krashen, S.D. *Principles and Practice in Secondary Language Acquisition*. Oxford: Pergamon Press, 1982.

Lado, R. *Language Teaching: A Scientific Approach*. Bombay: Tata MacGraw Publishing Co. Ltd. 51.

Leblanc, R. and G. Painchand. "Self-Assessment as a Second Language Placement Instrument." *TESOL Quarterly*. 1985, 673-87.

Leo, Van Lief. "Interaction in the Language Curriculum: Awareness, Autonomy and Authenticity" in *ELT Journal* Vol. 52/2, April 1998. Oxford University Press, 1998, 166.

Littlewood, W. *Communicative Language Teaching: An Introduction*. Cambridge: Cambridge University Press, 1981, 1.

Littlewood, W. *Foreign and Second Language Learning: Language Acquisition Research and its Implications for the Classroom*. Cambridge CVP. 1984, 1.

Long, M.H. and G. Crookes. "Intervention Points in Second Language Classroom Processes." Paper presented at *RELC Regional Seminar*, Singapore 21-26, April 1986.

Long, M.H. and P.A. Porter. "Group Work, Inter Language Talk and Second Language Acquisition." *TESOL Quarterly* 19(2), 1985, 207-28.

Lyons, J. (ed.). *New Horizons in Linguistics*. London: Penguin, 1970, 145.

Mackey, W.F. *Language Teaching Analysis*. London: Longman, 1965, 157.

Menon, T.K.N. and M.S. Patel. *The Teaching of English as a Foreign Language*. Baroda: Achariya Book Depot. 1957, 45. (eds.) 1979, 161.

Nunan, David. *Designing Task for the Communicative Classroom*. Cambridge: Cambridge University Press. 1989, 10.

Nunan, D. *The Learner-Centered Curriculum: A Study in Second Language Teaching*. Cambridge: Cambridge University Press, 1988.

Oskarsson, M. "Self-Assessment of Language Proficiency: Rationale and Applications." *Language Testing*, 6: 1989, 1-13.

Oxford, R. and M. Ehrman. "Second Language Research on Individual Differences" in *Annual Review of Applied Linguistics* 13, 188-205.

Pattison, P. *Developing Communication Skills*. Cambridge University Press, 1987.

Penny, *Ur. A Course in Language Teaching: Practice and Theory*. Cambridge: Cambridge University Press, 19.

Pittman, G. *Teaching Situational English*. London: Evans. 1963, 179.

Prabhu, N.S. "Procedural Syllabuses." Paper read at the *RELC Seminar* at Singapore, 1983.

Prabhu, N.S. *Second Language Pedagogy*. Oxford: Oxford University Press, 1987, 1-2.

Prasad, N.K. *The language Issue in India*. Leela Devi Publications: Delhi, 1979, 53.

Pride, J.B. and J. Holmes (eds.). *Sociolinguistic: Selected Readings*. Harmondsworth: Penguin Books, 1972, 278.

Prodoromon, Luk. "The Good Language Teacher." *English Teaching Forum* 29, 2: 2-7.

Revell, J. *Teaching Techniques for Communicative English*. London: Macmillan Publishers, 1979, 10-11.

Richards, J.C. and T.S. Rodgers. *Approaches and Methods in Language Teaching*. Cambridge: Cambridge University Press, 1986, 17.

Richards, J.C. and D. Nunan. *Second Language Teacher Education*. Cambridge: Cambridge University Press, 1990, 95.

Richterich, R. (ed.). *Case Studies in Identifying Language Needs*. Oxford: Pergamon Press, 1983.

Richterich, R. and J.L. Chancerel. *Identifying the Needs of Adults Learning a Foreign Language*. Council of Europe. Pergamon Press, 1980.

Rivers, W.R. "From Linguistic Competence to Communicative Competence" in *TESOL* Vol. 7, No. I, 1973, 28.

Rivers, W.R. "From Linguistic Competence to Communicative Competence" *in TESOL* Vol. 7, No. 1, 1993, 31-32.

Rivers, W.M. *The Psychologist and the Foreign Language Teacher:* Chicago and London: University of Chicago Press, 1964, 163.

Rivers, W.M. *Communicating Naturally in Second Language: Theory and Practice in Language Teaching*. Chicago: The University of Chicago Press, 1983, 43.

Roberts, J.T. "The Use of Dialogues for Teaching Transactional Competence in Foreign Language" *in ELT Documents* 12, 57.

Rubin & Jernudd (eds.). *Can Language Be Planned? Sociolinguistic Theory and Practice for Developing Nations.* Honolulus: The University Press of Hawon, 218.

Schwartz, B. "Permanent Education." *Final Report CCCIEP (77) 8* Revised 1977. 15.

Sheldon, L.E. (ed.). "ELT Textbooks and Materials Problems in Evaluation and Development." *ELT Documents* 126, 26-28.

Singh, R.K. "A Case of Syllabus Constraints in ELT." *The Journal of English Language Teaching* 17, 6: 187-92.

Sood, S.C. *New Directions in English Language and Literature Teaching in India.* Ajanta Publications, 1988, 108.

Stern, H.H., R. Rullmann *et al. Module Making: A study in the Development and Evaluation of Learning Materials for French as a Second Language*. Toronto: Ontario Ministry of Education, 1980, 60.

Stenhouse, L. *An Introduction to Curriculum Research and Development*. London: Heinemann, 1975, 86-7.

Stern, H.H. "Review and Discussion." *ELT Documents* 118, 8.

Stern, H.H. *Fundamental Concept of Language Teaching.* Oxford: Oxford University Press, 1983, 453.

Syal, Pushpinder. "The New Syllabus in Communication Skills in Punjab University and the Role of ELT Centre." *Focus on English*, 6, 1: 1990, 19-24.

Tonkyn, A. "Observations on Syllabus Reform." *Focus on English*, 4, 3: 21-27.

Trim, J.L.M. *Developing a Unit/Credit Scheme of Adult Language Learning*. Oxford: Pergamon Press, 1980.

Trim, J.L.M. *et al. Systems Development in Adults Language Learning: A European Unit/Credit System for Modern Language Learning by Adults*. Oxford: Pergamon Press, 1980.

Tubin, J. "What the Good Language Learner Can Teach Us." *TESOL Quarterly*, 1975, 41-51.

Tudor, I. *Learner-Centredness as Language Education.* Cambridge: Cambridge University Press. 1996, 128-29.

University Grants Commission. *Report of Curriculum Development Centre in English.* New Delhi, UGC, 1989, 328.

Van EK, J. and J.L.M. Trim. *Across the Threshold.* Pergamon Press. Council of Europe. 1984, 20.

Van EK, J. and S. Glass. "Target Language Input from Non-native Speakers." Paper presented at the Seventeenth Annual TESOL Convention, Toronto, 1983.

Verma, K. Shivendra. *Aspects of English Language Teaching: Focus on Functions.* T.R. Publications. 1993, 115-16.

Wagner, J. "Innovation in Foreign Language Teaching." *AILA Review* 5: 99-117.

Wenden, A. *Learner Strategies for Learner Autonomy.* Hemel Hempstead. Prentice Hall, 1991, 7.

Wenden, A. "What Do Second Language Learners Know about Their Language Learning? A Second Look at Retrospective Accounts." *Applied Linguistics*, 186-205.

Widdowson, H.G. *Explanations in Applied Linguistics.* Oxford: Oxford University Press, 1979, 248.

Widdowson, H.G. *Teaching Language as Communication.* Oxford: Oxford University Press, 1978, 18.

Widdowson, H.G. "Acquisition and Use of language Systems." *Applied Linguistics,* 1978, 10.

Widdowson, H.G. *Stylistics and the Teaching of Literature.* Longman, 1975, 17.

Willey, K.M. "Language Games" in W.R. Lee (ed.) *ELT Selections* 2: *Articles from English Language Teaching* London: Oxford University Press, 1967, 95.

Wilkins, D.A. *Notional Syllabuses.* London: Oxford University Press, 1976.

Yalden, J. The *Communicative Syllabus: Evolution, Design and Implementation.* Oxford: Pergamon Press, 1983.

Yalden, J. "An Interactive Approach to Syllabus Design: the Frameworks Project" in *ELT Documents* 124, 33.